The Politics of Division, Partition, and Unification

edited by
Ray Edward Johnston

The Praeger Special Studies program—utilizing the most modern and efficient book production techniques and a selective worldwide distribution network—makes available to the academic, government, and business communities significant, timely research in U.S. and international economic, social, and political development.

The Politics of Division, Partition, and Unification

PRAEGER SPECIAL STUDIES IN INTERNATIONAL POLITICS AND GOVERNMENT

JX
4055
.P64
West

Arizona State Univ. West Campus Library

Praeger Publishers　　New York　Washington　London

Library of Congress Cataloging in Publication Data
Main entry under title:

The Politics of division, partition, and unification.

(Praeger special studies in international politics and government)

1. Dismemberment of nations—Addresses, essays, lectures.   I. Johnston, Ray Edward.
JX4055.P64   320.1'5   75-23973
ISBN 0-275-55660-3

PRAEGER PUBLISHERS
111 Fourth Avenue, New York, N.Y. 10003, U.S.A.

Published in the United States of America in 1976
by Praeger Publishers, Inc.

All rights reserved

© 1976 by Praeger Publishers, Inc.

Printed in the United States of America

INTRODUCTION: TOWARD AN EMPIRICAL ANALYSIS OF POLITICAL PARTITION

The phenomenon of political partition enjoys both a broad contemporary scope and a lengthy historical lineage. A review of UN statistics, for example, shows that the world system is partitioned into 135 nation-states, and there are at least a dozen major treaty or trade blocs (e.g., NATO, CENTO, SEATO, OAS, OAU, Warsaw Pact, C of E, EEC, ECSC, EFTA, OECD, and COMECON).[1] Furthermore, the United States is an outstanding example of layers of partition, boasting thousands of legally partitioned units of government. There are 50 states, 3,049 counties, 18,048 municipalities, 17,105 townships, 21,264 special districts, 21,782 school districts.[2] Such partitioning of the world is not new, however. Any historian will point out that the practice is at least as old as the Assyrian Empire.

Despite its breadth and longevity there is a great deal of conceptual confusion about political partition, and there seem to have been few efforts to focus directly upon the subject as an empirical phenomenon. Few scholars have treated it as either an independent or dependent variable, and fewer still have produced typologies of partition or attempted to analyze forms and types of partitions qua partitions as political strategies. Though this article does not solve all these problems, it attempts to point out directions such empirical studies might take.

Our examination is organized into five major sections. The first of these is a review of the literature which relates to the study of partition as an instrument of politics, to theories of national and international integration, and to the study of war. The second section, dealing with the relationship between conflict and partition, is an extension of our review and presents a model which depicts partition and unification as the cause and outcome of conflict. In the third section (which we call "toward an empirical concept of partition"), the functional requisites of an integrated political system are utilized to derive an empirical definition of national partition and conversely a similar definition of national unification, which we discover might be better termed national amalgamation. The terms "national unification" and "national unity" might best be reserved to carry the

---

This essay originally appeared in the Columbia <u>Journal of International Affairs</u> 28, no. 2 (1973). Reprinted with permission.

concept of long-run development of a nation of people through the processes suggested by structural-functional and developmental theorists. Several hypothetical typologies of political partition are related to types and levels of conflict and to the functional requisites of an integrated political system. The fourth section treats our definition of national partition as the independent variable and lists a set of empirical propositions that can be asked in studies of partitioned nations today, as well as studies of historical political systems. The fifth and final section deals with a concluding note on the probability of peaceful reunification of divided nations. Here our prognosis is not optimistic, for we tend to agree with other theorists of national unity and integration that these are processes which require the combination of political authority and voluntary support over the long haul. Short-run reunification, like other forms of national unification, fits our earlier model of conflict, wars of conquest, and national amalgamation of diverse peoples. With this much by the way of introduction, we now turn to our review of the literature.

REVIEW OF LITERATURE RELATED TO THE STUDY OF PARTITION

After the "Great War" and the creation of the League of Nations, statesmen and scholars alike became increasingly concerned with the problems of world order, solidarity of nations, world integration, and world peace. As a consequence, academics have produced an enormous number of normative theories and case studies tending to support either the "nationalist" or the "internationalist" views of "partition" and "unity of nations."[3] Even the more recent work of Karl Deutsch, among other scholars of the post-World War II period, has its prescriptive characteristics.[4] Deutsch spells out a "political formula" for the integration of the European Community and, thereby, a formula for world order and integration. The scientific value of Deutsch's work and the works of such others as the neo-functionalists during the 1960s is their focus upon empirical and frequently operational variables.[5] Despite this heuristic value, they tend to be formulas to be utilized by national and international elites in the construction of world order or national integration. We have no interest in adding still another normative system of thought for world integration or national unification. Rather, we seek directions for a value-neutral, scientific analysis of political partition by which its causes and effects may be explained as empirical phenomena. In taking this approach, we assume that a scientific understanding of the political content of partition will contribute to a better understanding and more reasoned policies regarding it.

INTRODUCTION

It is a vain search of seminal works and texts in political science for index references to the terms of "partition," "unification," and "reunification." Even such simple and initial empirical propositions as the following seem to have escaped the attention of researchers.[6]

1. What is the statistical probability of reunification when partition is externally imposed on a homogeneous nation of people?
2. What is the statistical probability of internal struggles for partition when unification or amalgamation of heterogeneous communities of people has occurred?
3. As externally imposed partition varies from the subnational to the national and extra-national levels, what are the variations in the levels of intensity and the scope of conflict?

These three propositions, or at least the search for answers to them, raise the problem of conceptual clarity of partition as an analytic construct or empirical phenomenon. The propositions also suggest that the study of partition may be closely related to studies of imperialism, causes of war (both civil and internation), conflict resolution processes, and lower orders of internal strife and conflict.

CONFLICT AND PARTITION

Our survey of the historical literature, dating to the time when Lithuania stretched from the Baltic Sea to the Black Sea (circa 1559 A.D.), shows that there has not been one instance of the partition of a nation that was not followed by further conflict.[7] However, the participants in the conflict differ in relationship to the era of partition. Conversely, the research also shows that there has not been one instance of unification which has not also been preceded and succeeded by both internal and external conflict. These two findings, based perhaps on an all too cursory review, suggest that partition and unification may be two sides of the same coin, depending upon the ideological position one brings to the subject. This is also suggested by any reading and comparison of the early and recent twentieth century writings on nationalism, international law, and integration wherein the ideology of the actors tends to determine what is partition and what is unity. Partition to one party may be national self-determination to another and hence unification.

Furthermore, the distinction is not at all clear between the nation-state which claims to have resulted from partition and the nation-state which claims to have been a product of unification. As Francis G. Wilson so long ago observed:

> While national unity of the United States (rising from a revolution for national partition) was to be the product

> of blood and iron in the middle of the nineteenth century,
> as was the case with German and Italian unity, this was
> not so with French revolutionary idealism, which oscil-
> lated between imperialistic attainment of freedom and
> the maintenance of national unity. [8]

According to him, any group with nationalistic aspirations retains
the possible means of disintegrating the state. This, he claims, can
occur despite the fact that the "whole" has a tremendous advantage
over the dissenting group. Thus, we conclude that partition and unity
may be different sides taken by factions in a common quarrel.

Comparing the recent writings of Karl Deutsch and Claude Ake
to the earlier works of Wilson and C. J. H. Hayes, written immediately after World War I, we find that whenever the concept of the
integrated or unified state is used it is assumed to be applied to a
people of common race, language, culture, religion, historical experiences, and traditions. [9] From these assumptions, we can derive an
empirical concept of political partition that analyzes the political and
legal divisions of such common people. However, as C. J. H. Hayes
(among others) noted, whenever the concept of unity is applied to a
particular nation-state, one finds so many mixtures of stock (e. g.,
race, language, subcultures, religions, historical experiences, and
traditions) that it can hardly be said that there is a sovereign state
representing a homogeneous nation of people. [10] As a consequence,
we again refer to the idea that "partition" and "national unity" or
"unification" have been treated to date as ideological positions taken
by political parties in conflict as well as positions taken by the
scholars who have studied the conflict.

TOWARD AN EMPIRICAL CONCEPT OF PARTITION

Students of political integration, system change, development,
and national stability (read unification in almost every instance) suggest that certain requisite functions must be performed at some, as
yet unknown, level before one is able to speak of the sovereign state
or the "integrated system." These functions suggest, as we noted
above, the possibility of distinguishing between partition and amalgamation as nation-forming processes. The requisite functions are
as follows:
1. Some level of cultural homogeneity and value consensus must be
   attained.
2. An unknown scope and intensity of "social communication" is
   required.

3. This social communication is achieved by what has become known as social mobilization which is a process of breaking down old traditions and making the people available for new patterns of socialization, especially political socialization.
4. A uniformity of message content and cognitive agreement must be produced by mass media and educational institutions.
5. Economic interdependence between agrarian and urban people must be achieved by the development of a "common market place" or "national market place for distribution."
6. In addition, Claude Ake identified four structural characteristics of an "integrated" political system: (a) authoritarian—the government manifests a determination and ability to use its power (which is large, concentrated, and easily mobilized) to carry out its policies; (b) paternal—a political class (elite) willing and able to lead the non-coalescing majority; (c) identific—a mutual identity between the political class and the governed; and (d) consensual—the political class is solidary and the hegemony of the political class is not threatened by a counter-elite.[11]

Based on the above variables, national partition can be defined as the political and legal division into two or more politically bounded territories of people who, prior to such division, showed high positive scores on each of these functional requisites (variables). Conversely, we can define national amalgamation as the political bounding of a territory of people into a national state who, prior to claims of national autonomy, showed low scores on these same system variables.

By approaching the definition of national partition in terms of these empirical measurements, we may at least be able to examine historical political systems and isolate cases that approximate partition. Thereby, we can begin obtaining some initial answers to the questions of statistical probability regarding reunification posed at the beginning of this essay.

Both past and contemporary research shows that legal and political bounding of people into autonomous and semi-autonomous units varies from the international to the sub-national levels of the political system. For example, Zbigniew Brzezinski points out that the Soviet Union had dual intentions in controlling a partitioned Eastern Europe. First, these partitions provided both a defensive buffer and a strategically advanced jump-off point toward Western Europe. Next, according the Brzezinski, it satisfied the desire to create popularly accepted communist regimes in Eastern Europe.[12] At the sub-national level, Charles Moore, Ray Johnston, and Saadia Greenberg have conducted studies of "community control" and "school decentralization" and concluded that the white middle- and upper-class elites within United States cities have traditionally used legal partition as an insulation and divorcement device between emerging local elites as well as a cooptive or symbolic reward device.[13] Like the actions of the Soviet elites, the creation of locally partitioned groups in the United States generally serves as a buffer and as a creation of popularly accepted participation roles for the mass man within the urban polity.

It appears, therefore, that the existence of the national state eliminates neither the desire for political and legal partition nor the use of partition as an instrument to buffer the controlling classes from the demands of the governed. Rather, the existence of the national state seems to establish the canons of further partition. Again to draw from Hayes:

> A nationality may exist without an organized sovereign state of its own, and vice versa a political state may embrace several nationalities, though the tendency has been pronounced in modern times for every self-conscious nationality to aspire to political unity and independence.[14]

Claude Ake might also add to our discussion that

> [t]he pull of the traditional way of life does not always work to the disadvantage of the political class. For one thing, ethnic particularism helps make the political system more identific by helping to produce a pattern of segmentary political alignments cutting across the elite-mass gap, and thus keeping the political system from being dangerously polarized.[15]

Decentralization or sub-national partitioning to insulate the ruling class provides one of the mechanisms Ake prescribes when he admonishes the political class to give the governed some sense of having control over events; and as long as the governed somehow believe that government serves their interest, the legitimacy of the government is enhanced.[16]

Sub-national partitioning of peoples into semi-autonomous units is one vehicle the political class can use to monopolize power while imbuing the masses with a sense of having some control over their own lives. The appearance of mass participation in decision-making, Ake notes, must be kept up with great care, for, without it, a general feeling of helplessness tends to precipitate alienation. The latter may result in the further disintegration of the nation-state. Community control, local district, and class-based suburbs all provide some sense of mass participation in decision-making.[17]

INTRODUCTION

TABLE 1

Types of Legal and Political Partition

System Level	Type of Partition	
International or Supra-National	Blocs, Trade Regions, Treaty Organizations, etc.	
National	If Federal: Republics (e.g., USSR)	If Unitary: département
Sub-national	Counties Municipalities Special Districts (i.e., schools)	Counties or Prefects Municipaux

A useful concept of partition must be broad enough to isolate the phenomenon no matter where it occurs. Therefore, we have sketched an initial typology of the levels of political partition in Table 1. One way this typology might be utilized to shed light upon the problem of isolating national partition is the hypothetical juxtaposition of the integration variables of Claude Ake with the type and level of partition. We have done this for illustrative heuristic purposes in Table 2.

Suppose now that we allow the type of partition to vary according to the type of conflict that might produce it. Our typology of conflict is suggested by the recent work of scholars dealing with national and subnational conflict.[18] The typology in Table 3 is offered in an a priori fashion to empirical tests. Here we suggest that when conflict varies from the domestic legislative conflict among parties and ideological camps to that of international wars, such as World War II, the Korean War, and the Vietnam war, the type of partition used to settle the conflict varies from administrative decentralization of specific (managerial) powers to the division of spoils among the victors and contestants. Examples of the latter are the aftermath of the Congress of Vienna and its "redrawing the map of Europe" and the use of the 38th parallel to split a nation of people with a common

TABLE 2

The Probability of Homogeneity with Respect to Specified Requisites of Integration at Various System Levels of Partition

Type/level of Partition	Political System Requisite Variables							
	Culture	Social Communication	Political Socialization	Economic Interdependence	Authoritarian Elite	Paternal Elite	Identific Elite	Consensual Elite
Blocs and International Treaty Organizations	M	N	M	MH	N	N	N	M
Trade Regions International	M	N	N		MH	M	N	M
	MH	MH	MH				MH	H
Nation-States (Federal)	MH to H	MH to H	MH to H	MH to H	MH to H	MH to H	M to H	M
Nation-States (Unitary)	MH to H	MH to H	MH to H	M to H	H	MH to H		
Counties				MH to H	MH to H	MH to H	MH	H
Municipalities:								
(Urban)	MH to H	MH to H	MH to H	MH to H	N to H	N to H	N to H	N to H
(Rural)	H	H	H	H	N to H	N to H	N to H	N to H
School Districts	H	H	H	H	H	H	N to H	H

Note: H: Represents high probability of homogeneity of members with respect to system variable.
MH: Represents majority members homogeneous with respect to system variable.
M: Represents high probability of finding mixed orientations of members with respect to system variable.
N: Represents low probability of finding homogeneity of members with respect to system variable.

The qualitative values appearing in each cell are based on the intuition and learned guesses that the more local the level of partition, the more likely we will find homogeneity of members with respect to system variable. The N to H values at the municipal elite level are a product of the findings of Robert Agger and his associates. Their research indicates that at least U. S. communities vary from almost the absence of an elite group to the presence of a conspiratorial elite.19

INTRODUCTION

TABLE 3

Types of Political Partition Generated by Types and Levels of Conflict

Type of Conflict	Level of Conflict		
	Sub-National	National	International
Legislative and Party	Decentralization of specific powers		
Strikes and Protests	Decentralization of specific powers		
Riots	Decentralization of specific powers		
Revolution and Civil War		Nation-State	
Economic and Imperialistic		Amalgamation	Colonialism
International War			Division of Spoils: Congress of Vienna Korea Vietnam Germany
			Blocs: CMEA EEC NATO

culture, history, race, and language into two ideological camps, each of which claim political hegemony over their allotted territory and peoples.

TREATMENT OF PARTITION OF NATIONS AS AN INDEPENDENT VARIABLE

If we treat our earlier definition of national partition as the independent variable, the empirical comparative and interdisciplinary research might well focus on the following research questions and propositions:

I. Adaptive Social Behavior (Economy)
  A. As partition occurs, what impact does it have upon the economic commitments of the members?
  B. As partition occurs, what impact does it have upon the ratio of labor committed to agricultural pursuits and labor committed to industrial and professional economic roles?
  C. As partition occurs, what impact does it have upon the creation of credit and wealth of each part and of the former whole?

- D. As partition occurs, what changes, if any, evolve in the use of allocative mechanisms such as market price, hierarchy, bargaining, and brokerage?
- E. As partition occurs, what impact, if any, does it have upon the equitable distribution of wealth?
- F. As partition occurs, what impact, if any, does it have on aggregate international trade; upon each remnant's international trade; upon the need for international transfers of grants in aid?
- G. As partition occurs, what happens to the propensity for governmental intervention into the economy (e.g., the encouragement of enterprise, planning, economic innovation)?
- H. As partition occurs, what happens to the psychological commitments of members to economic roles?
- I. Is there a relationship between partition and the levels of the flow of goods and services between different parts of the newly formed nation(s)?
- J. Do these levels and flows of goods and services form patterns related to decisions in the social, integrative, and governmental sectors of society?

II. Pattern Maintenance (Social-Cultural Motivational Behavior and Structures)
- A. Is there any relationship between partition and changes in the family structure of the newly developed nation(s)?
- B. Is there a relationship between partition and urbanization or "rustification" of the population?[20]
- C. Is there any relationship between partition and changes in childhood socialization patterns?
- D. Is there a relationship between partition and levels and scope of political efficacy, political apathy, political alienation, and political hopelessness of the members of the nation(s)?
- E. Is there a relationship between partition and occurrence of domestic and social conflict?
- F. Is there a relationship between partition and the content and structure of child and adult education?
- G. Is there a relationship between partition and the use of police/military personnel to control social behavior?

III. Political Behavior and Governmental Structural Questions
- A. Institutional changes
    1. Is there a relationship between various forms of partition and types of structural changes in governmental institutions?
    2. Do both or all sides to a partition cling to past structures of government institutions or does each side change them in opposing directions?

INTRODUCTION

3. Do specific structural changes in government institutions precede partition?
4. How is partition related to political party structure and processes?
5. As partition occurs, is there a predictable change in the number of institutions wielding administrative power?
6. As partition occurs, is there predictable change in the relationships of central government with local governments?
7. Is there a relationship between partition and the number of communal redevelopment activities conducted by government and other politicized associations?

B. Political Elite Behavior
  1. Legitimation Behavior
    (a) Is there a relationship between the occurrence of partition and the propensity for those in power at the time of partition to define themselves as "fathers of the country" (i.e., paternalistic characteristics of office holders and political elite members)?
    (b) Is there a common pattern of rationalization of political elites of partitioned nations; that is to ask, are there commonalities of the "political formula" used by the political class in claiming the right to power? (This might be answered by socio-psychological analysis of the content of political formulas of opposing partitioned nations.)
    (c) Is there a relationship between the occurrence of partition and the constitutional checks on the political elite or ruling class?
  2. Elite Recruitment Behavior
    (a) Does the criteria of membership in the ruling class and the political elite change in predictable directions with national partition? (Here research might focus upon changes in both ascriptive and achievement criteria used in elite recruitment before and after partition.)
    (b) Does partition generally increase or decrease the numbers included in the general political class (i.e., those from whom party, governmental, and associational members are drawn)?
    (c) By comparing several cases of partition or sampling partitioned nations, will the authoritarian characteristics of the political elite significantly differ from those of "non-partitioned" nations?
    (d) Is there a relationship between, say, the permanency of partition and the coercive behavior of political elites?

IV. Integrative Behavior and Structural Questions
   A. Values
      1. As partition occurs, what happens to the normative structure, the values of the citizen members?
      2. Is there a relationship between the rate and content of changes in citizen values and scope of acceptance of the "political formula"?
      3. Is there a divergence of opposing partitioned national elites in selecting cultural symbols and historical experiences to maintain social solidarity?
      4. How does hostilization of opposing camps vary among different types of political partition?
      5. Following partition, to what extent and from which classes or groups in society is there a general acceptance of political leaders as diligent and honest servants of public interest?
      6. Is there a difference in public acceptance of the honesty and diligence of leaders who participated in the partition and those who came to power after partition?
      7. Are there predictable relationships between public attitudes that the political class members are unduly enjoying a large share of systemic rewards and the permanency of partition and elite replacement?
   B. Government Penetration of Integrative Structures
      1. Are there predictable patterns, magnitude and scope, of government expenditures on integrative infrastructures, such as communication systems, long term energy development systems, social welfare systems, as nations are partitioned?
      2. Is there a relationship between partition and the output of messages from the central government in ratio to the input of messages to the central government?
      3. Are there significant differences between elites of partitioned nations and elites of non-partitioned nations to rely more upon symbols of scientific rationality than upon mysticism and religion for integrative purposes?

Additional proposals for empirical and comparative work can be listed. All we want to do here is to suggest that when partition is treated as an empirical phenomenon and isolated, a great deal can be learned about human behavior by comparing opposing partitioned peoples as well as by comparing partitioned peoples to non-partitioned peoples. Most of these propositions are treated in the integration literature as normative prescriptions rather than empirical questions.[21]

INTRODUCTION xvii

A CONCLUDING NOTE ON UNIFICATION

In the United States, we have not yet begun to treat partition as an independent or dependent variable. Generally, we see units of government as the result of the machinations of historical accident or the "muddling-through" process. The difficulty with this approach is that very few legal-political boundaries occur by accident. Most of them are intended to solve some problem or allocate values and costs of the system. This essay then is a call for a closer look at the causes and effects of dividing different groups and classes of people into political units.

Institutional integration of non-political areas of life as well as extra-national and supra-national structures is well supported by recent research. Even the divided nations find it possible to cooperate in the areas of trade, cultural and family communication, and research. However, as Ernst Haas notes, integration in one institutional area is not necessarily accompanied by integration in another institutional area.[22] We also note that the multinational corporation may provide higher levels of integration of trade and social communication. However, we are skeptical about the peaceful reunification through the integrative processes of partitioned nations.

So far in the history of modern nations, with the exception perhaps of only the most primitive, unification has been the product of blood and iron. When we apply the above criteria of national partition and ask the question of how one might go about unifying a divided nation, we discover that most nations from Metternich's Austria to the United States are a product of conquest and amalgamation of diverse peoples. National unity, when it occurs, generally takes the long slow path of social mobilization of diverse peoples, as outlined by Claude Ake, Ernst Haas, and Karl Deutsch.[23] Korea is a case in point. Once (circa 1400) Korea consisted of three nations of people. Through military conquest and struggle a single nation was amalgamated and with 500 years of control by a continuous central political regime, a common history, culture, language, and economy was welded. This ended with Japanese conquest and the Korean war.

If, then, we speak frankly about the possibilities of unification, we conclude that current divided nations have two choices: to reunite by conflict and conquest or to peacefully co-exist and permit the slow process of social mobilization and integration of new nations to occur. Accordingly, the peaceful reunification of Germany or Korea appears unlikely, and Ireland, meanwhile, is in the throes of civil strife. Palestine struggles daily with the Arab nations to prevent military reunification, while Pakistan and Bangladesh can reunite only at the price of war. Therefore, talk of peaceful reunification of the politically partitioned nations becomes null and void

xviii THE POLITICS OF DIVISION, PARTITION, AND UNIFICATION

unless it deals with the development of new nations out of the old, and not the peaceful reunification of the old nation.

NOTES

1. United Nations Yearbook of National Accounts Statistics (New York: United Nations Statistical Office, 1970); United Nations Statistical Yearbook (New York: United Nations Statistical Office, 1970).

2. The United States Statistical Abstracts 1969, 90th ed. (Washington, D. C.: U. S. Bureau of the Census, 1969).

3. The normative theories and case studies supporting the nationalist school of thought in relatively recent literature on the subject of new nations, the concern for and about "national stability," and "national integration" are represented by the following works: Karl W. Deutsch, Nationalism and Social Communication (New York: John Wiley & Sons, 1953); William Kornhauser, The Politics of Mass Society (Glencoe, Ill.: Free Press, 1959); Lucien Pye, Politics, Personality, and Nation Building (New Haven, Conn.: Yale University Press, 1962); Rupert Emerson, From Empire to Nation (Cambridge, Mass.: Harvard University Press, 1960); Carlton J. Hayes, Nationalism: A Religion (New York: Atherton Press, 1963); J. H. Kautsky, Political Change in Underdeveloped Countries: Nationalism and Communism (New York: John Wiley & Sons, 1962); Hans Kohn, Nationalism: Its Meaning and History (Princeton, N. J.: Van Nostrand, 1955); John Herz, "Rise and Demise of the Territorial States," World Politics 9, no. 4 (July 1957): 473-93; Leonard W. Doob, "From Tribalism to Nationalism in Africa," Journal of International Affairs 16, no. 2 (Fall 1962): 144-55 (this entire issue of the Journal dealt with nation-building as the order of the day). Going further, to the concerns of the 1960s with national stability, we find such works as: Kenneth Waltz, "Stability of the Bipolar World," Daedalus 93, no. 3 (Summer 1964): 881-909; Karl W. Deutsch and J. David Singer, "Multipolar Power Systems and International Stability," World Politics 16, no. 3 (April 1964): 390-406; Dina A. Zinnes, "The Requisites of International Stability," Journal of Conflict Resolution 8, no. 3 (September 1964): 301-05; Michael Haas, "Types of Asymmetry within Social and Political Systems," General Systems 12 (1967): 69-80, and his "International Subsystems: Stability and Polarity," American Political Science Review 64, no. 1 (March 1970): 98-122. This list does not exhaust the literature; it merely points in the direction of recent scholarship that is both normative, on the one hand, and descriptive or empirical, on the other, and which tends to prescribe the stable national state as the "telos" of politics. The internationalist

position is well reviewed in Inis L. Claude, Jr.'s Swords Into Plowshares (New York: Random House, 1959) and Power and International Relations (New York: Random House, 1962). In the latter work, Claude reviews the following (from which we have drawn our own knowledge of the "internationalist" point of view): Otto Nathan and Heinz Norden, eds., Einstein on Peace (New York: Simon and Schuster, 1960); Gilbert McAllister, ed., World Government: The Report of the First London Parliamentary Conference (London: The Parliamentary Group for World Government, 1952); Everett Lee Millard, Freedom in a Federal World (New York: Oceana, 1961); A. C. Ewing, The Individual, the State, and World Government (New York: Macmillan, 1947); Lester B. Pearson, "The Present Position of the United Nations," International Relations, no. 8 (October 1957): 327-42; Grenville Clark and Luis B. Sohn, World Peace Through World Law (Cambridge, Mass.: Harvard University Press, 1960); Ernst Haas, "'The Uniting of Europe' and the Uniting of Latin America," Journal of Common Market Studies 5, no. 4 (June 1967): 315-43; Ernst Haas and Philippe Schmitter, "Economics and Differential Patterns of Political Integration: Projects About Unity in Latin America," International Organization 18, no. 4 (Autumn 1964): 705-37; Ernst Haas, The Uniting of Europe (Stanford, Calif.: Stanford University Press, 1958); also see Barry B. Hughes and John E. Schwarz, "Dimensions of Political Integration and the Experience of the European Community," International Studies Quarterly 16, no. 3 (September 1974): 263-94, for a review of the integrationist empirical findings. Our point in this rather lengthy note is that the nationalists and internationalists have made common theoretical assumptions and adopted common methodological frameworks; consequently, their data and inferences are biased toward an integrationist value position.

  4. Karl Deutsch, Political Community at the International Level (New York: Doubleday, 1954); see also his Political Community and the North Atlantic Area (Princeton, N.J.: Princeton University Press, 1957). Much of the theoretical literature on the study of regional integration is surrounded by problems of definition and conceptual imprecision. Indeed, one writer has noted quite succinctly that the study of this phenomenon may be placed in Thomas Kuhn's pre-paradigm stage of the development of science [see Kuhn's The Structure of Scientific Revolutions (Chicago: University of Chicago Press, 1962)]. For example, see James Caporaso, "Theory and Method in the Study of International Integration," International Organization 25, no. 2 (Spring 1971): 228-53. Ernst Haas' original and rather ambiguous concept of "spill-over" has its prescriptive characteristics, which he later refines with the empirical discovery that functional contexts are autonomous; see also Ernst B. Haas,

Beyond the Nation State (Stanford, Calif.: Stanford University Press, 1964) and his article "International Integration," in Limits and Problems of European Integration (The Hague: Martinus Nijhoff, 1963).

5. Michael Banks, in his "Systems Analysis and the Study of Regions," International Studies Quarterly 13, no. 4 (December 1969): 335-60, presents a general review of the recent literature dealing with (1) prescriptive and normative problems of world order, (2) empirical studies of regional security and world peace, (3) descriptive studies of regional structures, and (4) debate about merits of regional as opposed to universal interaction. In this and other reviews, Deutsch, Ernst Haas, Bruce Russet, Joseph Nye, and others are sometimes shown to emphasize either different data or different methodologies, but each is primarily concerned with world order and world integration. Sometimes Deutsch and his students are distinguished from Ernst Haas and his students by the claim that the former are more concerned with social communication research while the latter are more concerned with functional (i.e., institutional) areas of interaction.

6. This is not to fail to recognize the more rigorous refinements of the early work of Karl Deutsch. Morton Kaplan, for example, considers integration as a system of regulatory processes tying nations and organizations within a common framework in his Systems and Process in International Politics (New York: John Wiley & Sons, 1959), p. 98. Amitai Etzioni suggests that the essential conditions for integration exist when there is a supra-national agency disposing of a monopoly of power and occupying the center of decision-making; see his Political Unification: A Comparative Study of Leaders and Forces (New York: Holt, Rinehart & Winston, 1969), p. 16. Philip E. Jacob and Henry Teune focused upon the impact of values and habits in the integrative process in their "The Integrative Process: Guidelines for Analysis of Bases of Political Community," in The Integration of Political Communities, eds., Philip E. Jacob and James Toscano (New York: J. B. Lippincott, 1964). William E. Fisher actually constructed an empirical measure of integration in "An Analysis of the Deutsch Socio-Causal Paradigm of Political Integration," International Organization 23, no. 2 (Spring 1969): 254-90. See also Joseph Nye, "Comparative Regional Integration: Concept and Measurement," International Organization 22, no. 4 (Autumn 1968): 855-80, and his "Comparing Common Markets," in Regional Integration: Theory and Research, eds., Leon Lindberg and Stuart Scheingold (Cambridge, Mass.: Harvard University Press, 1971), pp. 260 ff.; James Caporaso, "Fisher's Test of Deutsch's Socio-Causal Paradigm of Political Integration: A Research Note," International Organization 25, no. 1 (Winter 1971): 120-31; Norman Thomas Uphoff and W. F. Illchman, Political Economy of Change

(Berkeley: University of California Press, 1971); James Rosenau, *The Adaptation of National Societies: A Theory of Political System Behavior and Transformation* (New York: McCaleb Seiler, 1970); and Phillipe Schmitter, "Central American Integration: Spill-Over, Spill-Around, or Encapsulation?," *Journal of Common Market Studies* 9, no. 1 (September 1970): 1-48. These scholars have all attempted more rigorous conceptualization and empirical measurements of particular variables related to the so-called integrative process than did the earlier theorists.

7. Some readers may take post-World War II Austria to be the exception. However, our cursory review of Austrian history since 1282 suggests that the most recent partition of Austria occurred following World War I in 1918. Since that time, Austria was further partitioned and then reamalgamated into the German Reich on 18 March 1938, by Hitler. At the conclusion of the World War II, with the Allied occupation, the Austrian Republic was reborn with Dr. Karl Renner's Constitutional government of 1 May 1945. By 15 September 1945, all three occupational forces recognized this government. Hence the war was the conflict that repartitioned Austria from Germany. The present state still leaves many of the pre-war partition problems (e.g., South Tyrol and the Danube) unsolved. Kurt Waldheim, *The Austrian Example* (New York: Macmillan, 1971); Hienrich Siegler, *Austria: Problems and Achievements Since 1945* (Bonn: Siegler, 1969); William B. Bader, *Austria Between East and West, 1945-1955* (Stanford, Calif.: Stanford University Press, 1966); Frederick C. Engelman, "Haggling for Equilibrium: The Renegotiation of the Austrian Coalition, 1959," *American Political Science Review* 56, no. 3 (September 1962): 651-62.

8. Francis Graham Wilson, *The Elements of Modern Politics* (New York: McGraw-Hill, 1936), p. 404.

9. The early literature used both "unified state" and "integrated state" as synonymous terms. We have done so here recognizing that recent development of the concept of integration goes much further than the concepts of political unification in describing social, economic, and political collective action to promote mutual interests.

10. C. J. H. Hayes, *Essays on Nationalism* (New York: Macmillan, 1926), pp. 1-35, and his *Historical Evolution of Modern Nationalism* (New York: Russell & Russell, 1931), passim.

11. Claude Ake, *A Theory of Political Integration* (Homewood, Ill.: Dorsey Press, 1967), pp. 96-116.

12. Zbigniew Brzezinski, *Alternative to Partition: For a Broader Conception of America's Role in Europe* (New York: McGraw-Hill, 1965), p. 16.

13. Charles H. Moore and Ray E. Johnston, "School Decentralization, Community Control and the Politics of Public Education," in

Urban Affairs Quarterly 6, no. 4 (June 1971): 421-45, and Saadia R. Greenberg and R. E. Johnston, "Parent Demands and School Decentralization in Detroit," Urban and Social Change Review 6, no. 1 (Fall 1972): 16-21.

    14. Hayes, Essays, op. cit., p. 5.
    15. Ake, Political Integration, op. cit., pp. 108-10.
    16. Ibid., p. 110.
    17. Ibid., p. 107.
    18. Representatives of some of the recent work on national and subnational conflict related to decentralization and partition are the following: William Gamson, Power and Discontent (Homewood, Ill.: Dorsey Press, 1968); Ted Gurr and Charles Ruttenberg, The Conditions of Civil Violence: First Tests of a Causal Model (Princeton, N.J.: Research Monograph 28, Center of International Studies, Princeton University, 1967); Lewis Coser, The Functions of Social Conflict (New York: Free Press, 1956); Alan A. Altschuler, Community Control (New York: Pegasus, 1970); Marilyn Gittell, Participants and Participation: A Study of School Policy (New York: Praeger, 1967); Mayer Zald, "Decentralization—Myth vs. Reality," in Public Administration, eds., Robert Golembiewski, et al. (Chicago: Rand McNally, 1966).
    19. Robert Agger, et al., The Rulers and the Ruled (New York: John Wiley & Sons, 1966).
    20. Pi-chao Chen, "Overurbanization, Rustication of Urban-Educated Youths, and Politics of Rural Transformation," Comparative Politics 4, no. 3 (April 1972): 361-86.
    21. While we have already cited much of the literature on integration at the national and international levels which we consider to have normative content, the reader may want to read Stuart A. Scheingold, "The North Atlantic Area as a Policy Arena," International Studies Quarterly 15, no. 1 (March 1971): 32-65, for his analysis of Karl Deutsch's prescriptive concern with cohesion and Ernst Haas's prescriptive concern with allocative structures.
    22. See Ake, Political Integration, op. cit.; Ernst Haas, "International Integration," op. cit.; and Deutsch, Political Community at the International Level, op. cit.
    23. Ernst Haas, "International Integration," op. cit.

CONTENTS

	Page
INTRODUCTION: TOWARD AN EMPIRICAL ANALYSIS OF POLITICAL PARTITION	v
LIST OF TABLES	xxiv

Chapter

1 A HOSTAGE OF HISTORY: NORTHERN IRELAND AND THE ISSUE OF INTEGRATION VERSUS UNIFICATION
 Thomas Hachey 1

2 DIVIDED BERLIN: ONE PAST AND THREE FUTURES
 Richard L. Merritt 17

3 SOCIALIZATION AND INTEGRATION STRATEGIES: THE CASE OF THE FEDERAL REPUBLIC OF GERMANY AND THE GERMAN DEMOCRATIC REPUBLIC
 Arthur M. Hanhardt, Jr. 40

4 INTERNATIONAL INTEGRATION THEORIES AND PROBLEMS OF UNIFYING A DIVIDED NATION: THE CASE OF KOREA
 Young Whan Kihl 55

5 UNIFICATION OR CONFRONTATION: AN ASSESSMENT OF FUTURE RELATIONS BETWEEN MAINLAND CHINA AND TAIWAN
 Yung Wei 67

6 BANGLADESH: THE PRICE OF NATIONAL UNITY
 Kathleen Knight 80

ABOUT THE EDITOR AND CONTRIBUTORS 99

LIST OF TABLES

Table		Page
1	Types of Legal and Political Partition	xi
2	The Probability of Homogeneity with Respect to Specified Requisites of Integration at Various System Levels of Partition	xii
3	Types of Political Partition Generated by Types and Levels of Conflict	xiii
4	Political Interest Among GDR Youth	45
5	Concept of Freedom Among GDR Youth	46
6	The Divided Nations: Comparative Data on Territory, Population, GNP, and Per Capita Income	71
7	Mainland China Versus Taiwan: A Comparison of Standard of Living (1969–70)	74

The Politics of Division, Partition, and Unification

CHAPTER 1

A HOSTAGE OF HISTORY: NORTHERN IRELAND AND THE ISSUE OF INTEGRATION VERSUS UNIFICATION

Thomas Hachey

In an age that has become almost accustomed to widespread violence and frequent disorders, Northern Ireland still confounds the attempts of outside observers to understand the nature of the conflict in that troubled land. Commentators have variously described the problem as racial, cultural, religious, economic. Indeed, Ulster's anxieties, frustrations and hatreds, generated by a combination of all of these factors, had festered for centuries before erupting with genocidal fury in 1969. Any real comprehension of the contemporary crisis in Northern Ireland, therefore, requires some appreciation of the historical origins and evolution of that community's divisive legacy.

Northern Ireland became a political entity in 1920, at a time when national boundaries were being redrawn in many parts of Europe, and when a number of long-suppressed ethnic groups were establishing new and autonomous states. Against that backdrop, the creation of Northern Ireland might simply appear as a generic element of the nationalist wave then sweeping Europe, or perhaps as but another political concession by an imperial government to a local demand for self-government. But neither of these views contains much merit. It would be more correct to say that the six northeastern counties of Ireland were fused into a political unit and accorded a government of their own, not because any part of the native population desired, let alone demanded, such an arrangement, but because the British government deemed it to be the most plausible way of reconciling the rival aspirations of the two Irish parties: the Nationalist (and mainly Roman Catholic) majority, who agitated for self-government for the whole country, and the Unionist (and mainly Protestant) minority, who insisted that Ireland remain within the United Kingdom. But in the region which comprises present-day Ulster, the Unionists constitute two-thirds of the population. Hence, Northern Ireland came into being not because a majority of the people in the area were nationalists, but rather because their opposition to nationalism had to be somehow neutralized.[1]

The forces which produced this paradoxical state of affairs can be traced far back into Irish history, and form a complicated pattern; the most essential points of this evolution, however, can be stated fairly readily.[2] Since the Reformation, which left Ireland Catholic when England became Protestant, religion has been a major dividing line in Irish politics. Perhaps Ireland's geographical proximity to the territorially larger and more populous English nation would have led in any case to the latter's treating the former as a client state,[3] but the anti-Catholic zeal of English sovereigns since Tudor times destroyed irrevocably any chance that might ever have existed for more amicable Anglo-Irish relations. Indeed, Catholicism became a symbol of a besieged Irish way of life during the survival conflict between the Gaelic and invading Anglo-Saxon cultures in the sixteenth and seventeenth centuries. Since Ulster clan chiefs raised the most effective opposition to religious and political Anglicization, their province was a natural target for English mercantilists who, with immigrant Scotch Presbyterian tillers as allies, dispossessed the native Irish of their property.[4] Moreover, Ulster's fertile lands and natural harbor facilities appealed to the plantation and commercial interests of the invaders. This tactic left Ulster as the only province in Ireland with a significantly large Protestant garrison. Although the Protestants were a minority in nearly every part of the country, they long enjoyed a virtual monopoly of power.

The Catholic majority in Ireland, formed from a mixture of the old Gaelic stock with English settlers of the medieval period in whom Gaelic cultural influence was very strongly marked, never reconciled itself to the political or economic dominance of the Protestant ascendancy. But Irish Catholic antipathy toward Britain only became a source of concern to the latter when Ireland in 1588 gave its sympathy and support to England's mortal enemy, Spain, when Irish partisans lent assistance to Charles I in the English Civil War, and later to James II following the Glorious Revolution of 1688. On each of these three occasions, Catholic Ireland's treachery, or involvement in British domestic rivalries, succeeded in convincing both the English government and the Protestant ascendancy in Ireland that the country's majority was a threat to the security of the realm. Accordingly, the Protestant-dominated Anglo-Irish parliament in Dublin, with London's consent and encouragement, passed penal legislation during the last few years of the seventeenth and early decades of the eighteenth century. The effect of this legislation was to strip the Catholic majority of all its political liberties, and many of its civil liberties, which turned the larger number of these people into craven, demoralized, dehumanized and impoverished serfs.[5]

Irish Protestant attitudes gradually began to change in the eighteenth century. The Anglo-Irish, more secure in their positions of power, less frightened of the beaten Catholic masses, resentful of British mercantilist commercial restrictions, and anxious to free the Irish parliament from English domination, developed a patriotism of their own. Active opposition was made possible when France joined the American colonies in their war against England, a development which provided those who sought it an excuse to form a volunteer Protestant army on the pretext of protecting Irish shores from a French invasion. With the leverage obtained from this armed militia, the Protestant Irish nationalist leader, Henry Grattan, demanded and received trade concessions and an independent Irish Parliament. But despite some mitigation of the penal laws and the spirit of tolerance associated with the Enlightenment, the Grattan group represented moderate Protestant reformers who thought only an educated Catholic elite should participate in the governance of the country and that any assimilation of the Catholic masses must await their political maturation.[6]

Theobald Wolfe Tone's Society of United Irishmen, however, represented the far left of the nationalist reform movement and found its inspiration in the French Revolution. As that revolution moved left, they kept pace, finally demanding a democratic republic. United Irishmen thought of themselves as culturally Irish, not as transplanted Britons or as Protestants. Many of the organization's adherents, especially those from the professional and commercial classes, felt the exploitation of an ascendancy controlled by aristocratic landed gentry who supported English mercantilist policies. In their determination to end this aristocratic dominance and British influence, United Irishmen looked upon the exploited Catholic peasantry as excellent revolutionary potential, allies of the Presbyterian and Nonconformist middle class. England was already at war with France in 1798 when the United Irishmen attempted to overthrow British rule in Ireland through an uncoordinated plan of rebellion which was to receive the assistance of a French fleet with an invading force.[7] In the disastrous risings of 1798, Protestants in Armagh and Antrim died no differently than Catholics in Wexford and Mayo. The significance of the United Irishmen movement lies in the fact that it represented the last Irish nationalist movement which was nonsectarian. Many Catholics supported it because they had grown impatient with the tokenism or gradualism of Protestant reformers; and they also shared the economic and political interests of Nonconformist nationalists who sought the overthrow of the ascendancy.

A major factor contributing to the failure of the United Irishmen movement was that most Irish Protestants preferred retention of the ascendancy, with all its shortcomings, to the extension of political equality to the Catholic majority. Moreover, limited Catholic gains toward equality, the fear of a French invasion supported by an Irish conspiracy, and the influence of the evangelical movement in Britain and Ireland, with its antinational thrusts and fundamentalist dogma, revived militant Protestantism and provided the Established Church and Nonconformity with a common no-popery position. The success of the Orange Order in the late 1790s was a manifestation of this new Protestant spirit. Orangeism was the outgrowth of an Ulster Protestant tenant-farmer secret society, the Peep O'Day Boys, rivals of the Defenders, a Catholic agrarian secret society. Protestant farmers resented papist competition for the limited land available, particularly in Ulster communities with large Catholic populations.[8] Beginning in 1795, the Orange Order grew rapidly in size and was soon terrorizing Catholics in southern Ulster counties, driving them into the western hinterlands of Connaught. Recognizing the antirevolutionary potential of the Orangemen, members of the gentry took command of the movement, armed its membership, and persuaded government authorities that no-popery was an effective tool of law and order. Orangeism spread throughout Ireland where it won adherents in the highest quarters, including members of the royal family. Comparable to Anglo-Saxon nationalist movements in both England and America, Orangeism remains today a vital force in the power structure in Northern Ireland: a divisive, irrational, hate movement in Irish life.[9]

England finally decided that Ireland's capacity for posing a threat to British security should no longer be tolerated and, rather than grant home rule to the Dublin parliament as a number of Whig politicians had hitherto suggested, the Westminster Parliament proposed to incorporate Ireland into the United Kingdom. Most of the landed Anglo-Irish gentry favored the Act of Union which became a reality in 1800, particularly since it accorded the Irish a more than generous number of seats at Westminster. But the Orange leaders at first opposed the parliamentary connection with Britain, fearing that a remote British parliament might be more responsive to Irish Catholic grievances and agitations. During the nineteenth century, however, Ulster Protestants became the most militant champions of maintaining the Union. Their sentiment changed as they came to appreciate that the maintenance of this union was the best guarantee of Protestant ascendancy in Ireland. Indeed, that conviction was confirmed when, in 1829, Catholics were admitted to full political rights, and when Daniel O'Connell subsequently created modern Irish nationalism on the foundation of Catholic civil rights. Because Ulster was the only section of Ireland to participate in the Industrial Revolution, as linen factories and the Belfast shipyards were assimilated into the British urban industrial complex, Protestant merchants and industrialists adopted the view that a revived Irish parliament reflecting the will of a clerically dominated peasant democracy would destroy Ulster's economy and persecute their religion. The prospect that Irish Protestants, instead of forming part of a permanent Protestant majority in the United Kingdom, would comprise a lasting minority in Ireland, made Orangemen militant champions of maintaining the Union.

In their opposition to nationalism the Irish Protestants had the consistent support of the Conservative party, and this made them a powerful force in British politics. But in Ireland itself, though they commanded a social and economic influence out of all proportion to their numbers, the only area in which their policy enjoyed widespread popular support was in the province of Ulster. After 1886, when Parnell and Gladstone concluded an alliance between Irish nationalism and British Liberalism, British Conservatives used Ulster opposition to Irish Home Rule as a weapon with which to maintain power and frustrate Liberalism. British Conservatives in Parliament and in the army endorsed and encouraged Ulster Protestant threats of civil war in order to defeat the constitutional inevitability of Home Rule. Liberal Prime Minister Herbert Asquith had promised the nationalist Irish Parliamentary Party that England would grant Home Rule to Ireland in return for the IPP's support of the Liberals' legislative goals at Westminster. The Irish kept their bargain by helping to reduce significantly the constitutional prerogatives of the House of Lords, long a Conservative bastion. Asquith, however, proved unable to implement Home Rule even though it was demonstrably the will of the majority of the British electorate. Faced with the threat of a rebellion by armed Ulster Protestant militia, and a mutiny among British army officers, the Liberal Prime Minister asked, and Irish Parliamentary Party leader John Redmond agreed, to postpone Home Rule when war with Germany erupted in August 1914.[10]

In order to obtain Irish nationalist support for the war effort, Home Rule was placed on the statute books, but the Liberal Government sought to appease Unionists with a suspensory bill delaying the operation of Home Rule until after the war was over. Britain thereby managed narrowly to escape a constitutional crisis, and possibly a civil war. But the Irish problem had not been solved; it had only been postponed once more. That not all Irish nationalists trusted the English government to honor its pledge, or approved of John Redmond's example of supporting the British war effort, became evident on Easter Monday 1916 when about 1,500 armed insurrectionists seized strategic positions throughout the city of Dublin and their leader, Padraic Pearse, announced the establishment of an Irish Republic.

British troops suppressed the rebellion in a week of bloody fighting that left the heart of the Irish capital in ruins.

The majority of Irishmen condemned Pearse and his Sinn Fein republican followers as a fanatical and traitorous lot, a not surprising sentiment in view of the fact that a quarter of a million Irishmen served voluntarily in the British army during World War I and their families supported them if not their cause. Yet, reprisal was the immediate response of the English government to the Rising. It was a tactic which would be repeatedly employed over the decades by the British in Ireland, almost always with disastrous results. The senseless execution of fourteen Irish republican leaders transformed the "dirty traitors" of Easter week into gallant martyrs and national heroes when imprisonment almost certainly would have doomed them to obscurity. England further antagonized Irish Catholic opinion in 1918 when, with manpower resources seriously depleted by the war with Germany, the British parliament authorized Prime Minister Lloyd George to extend conscription to Ireland.

Another act in the drama followed the Armistice of November 11, 1918, when it became evident how completely the nationalist movement had been seized by the extremists. In the British general election of December 1918, Irish Parliamentary Party "Home Rulers" were politically destroyed by the republican Sinn Fein party which swept every parliamentary seat outside Ulster except four. Hailing their victory as a mandate from the Irish people, the republicans refused to take their seats at Westminster and met instead, on January 21, 1919, at Dublin's Mansion House where Easter Rising veteran Eamon de Valera and fellow Sinn Feiners ratified the Irish Republic which had been proclaimed in 1916. Thereafter, from early 1919 to May 1921, the country was convulsed by full-scale hostilities between armed Irish republicans and British military forces. Meanwhile, confronted by the intransigence of British Protestant fanatics, and pressured by opportunist Conservative politicians, a Liberal government sold out its Irish nationalist allies by accepting partition as the final solution to the Irish Question.

In 1920, at the height of the Irish War for Independence, Prime Minister Lloyd George attempted to pacify the situation with a Government of Ireland bill, creating one parliament for six counties of northeast Ulster and another for the rest of Ireland. The partition scheme was debated for a year in the British Parliament and became law, after it received royal assent, on December 22, 1920. Ulster Protestants were by no means elated with this development for it was not the kind of settlement they had wanted. They had resisted home rule for Ireland; but they had never demanded home rule for themselves. What they had demanded was that they should remain as they were, that, whatever happened to the rest of Ireland, Ulster should remain as an undifferentiated part of the United Kingdom.

Nationalists responded to the British partition scheme by intensifying their guerrilla war in Ireland, but time was running out for both sides. The British government found itself besieged by appeals from some of its own citizens, and many others in America, Europe, and from all parts of the empire called for an end to the terror and reprisals in Ireland. For its part, the Irish Republican Army was facing critical shortages of men and armaments; the latter especially had become so depleted that the I.R.A. was scarcely able to engage in anything more than harassment by early 1921. Moreover, the people of the towns and countryside upon whose support, or at least indifference, the guerrillas depended, were growing increasingly weary of the long and costly war of attrition. Their physical and psychological endurance had reached the breaking point. An armistice was agreed to in May and negotiations, extending over several months, were held in London. Finally, in December, 1921, Prime Minister Lloyd George informed Arthur Griffith, Michael Collins and the other Irish representatives that political circumstances would not permit him to abandon Northern Ireland. He promised, however, that an official boundary commission would be formed whose task it would be to modify the size of Northern Ireland so that areas with large Catholic majorities would be included in the Irish Free State. But the boundary commission did not meet until 1924, when Lloyd George was no longer prime minister, and that body declared that it had no intention of threatening the existence of Northern Ireland. This destroyed all possibility for either a united Ireland or for the transfer of districts with Catholic majorities from the Six Counties to the Irish Free State. Several years of unsuccessful bargaining for the annexation of Ulster's Roman Catholic areas finally led Irish Free State representatives, in an agreement signed in London in 1925, to recognize the boundary of Northern Ireland. In return, the English government relieved the Irish Free State of its obligation to contribute to the British war debt. Republicans regarded the agreement as a betrayal of their cause but the majority of the Free State Irish accepted it as providing the best possible terms that could be obtained at that time.[11]

Eamon de Valera's victory in the Irish Free State elections of February 1932 signalled the beginning of a concerted effort by the Dublin government to sever all remaining ties with Britain. The oath of allegiance to the English crown was abolished, the governor-general was removed, and Ireland's attitude toward the empire was defined in the External Relations Act of 1936. The latter provided for a tenuous link between a de facto republic and the self-governing members of the British Commonwealth. Section three "authorized" the British king, with the permission of the Irish government, to act for the purpose of appointing international representatives and to conclude Irish international agreements. De Valera's formula of external association was essentially a device for asserting Ireland's complete sovereignty without outraging Great Britain beyond the limits of prudence. Consequently, the Irish Constitution of 1937, although proclaiming Dublin's authority over the whole island of Ireland, reflected a desire to consolidate recent gains rather than maneuver for the immediate end to partition.[12]

Ending partition remained de Valera's major unfinished task. He was opposed to the formal declaration of an Irish Republic precisely because he feared such a step might serve only to perpetuate the division. When World War II began, de Valera declared that Ireland would remain neutral for the duration of the conflict. The vast majority of his countrymen supported de Valera in his insistence that Ireland would not join any campaign for democratic freedom and self-determination so long as Ulster remained under English rule. Appeals from both Prime Minister Churchill and President Franklin Roosevelt had no effect upon the Irish determination to remain out of the war although morally the Irish people supported the Allied cause. Indeed, theirs was a one-sided neutrality in which British airmen who parachuted from disabled planes into Ireland were returned safely to England, while German airmen were interned for the remainder of the war. Moreover, 30,000 Irish recruits voluntarily served in the British armed services. Germany accepted Ireland's partisan neutrality since the Irish at least denied the use of their ports to the British navy. In the North, some Catholics frustrated by poverty and oppression hoped for a German victory as the only avenue to reunion with the South; and doubtlessly there were those in the South who, in the early months of the war, enjoyed seeing England in the role of the oppressed. Popular attitudes were simplified, however, when the Germans began bombing Belfast. Pro-British leanings also grew stronger when, on two occasions in May 1942, German bombs fell on Dublin by mistake.

Paradoxically, the final severance of the last link between Eire and the British Commonwealth was accomplished by a Dublin government dominated by that Irish party which had always advocated closer relations with Great Britain. Ireland's first postwar election was held in 1948 and, after 16 consecutive years in power, de Valera's Fiama Fail party was defeated. A coalition government under the leadership of John Costello, whose Fine Gael party was the heir to the pro-treaty leaders who, in 1922, had fought de Valera's anti-treaty forces, now emerged as the proponent of a Republic of Ireland Bill in the Irish parliament. It was an extraordinary volte-face by men of the old Michael Collins-William Cosgrove tradition, and the situation was made all the more bizarre by the opposition of de Valera and other life-long republicans. The latter insisted that by breaking the link with the Commonwealth, the Republic of Ireland Act would make the ending of partition much more difficult. Costello argued that the formal establishment of an Irish Republic was necessary to remove the ambiguities in the constitutional position and, when it came to the vote, Fianna Fail had no choice, in view of its record, but to support the government.

If the Irish government had chosen to combine the status of a sovereign republic with membership in the Commonwealth, as India had done, the practical obstacles to eventual unification would have been far less formidable than they were to become following Ireland's complete separation from the Commonwealth. The British government responded to the Dublin parliament's unilateral action with the Ireland Act of 1949 which retained anomalous privileges that have no counterpart in relations between Britain and other independent states. Fortunately for the Republic, the Irish continued to be invested with the same rights and obligations as other citizens of the United Kingdom. But the new British legislation also contained a pledge to Ulster:

> That Northern Ireland remains part of His Majesty's Dominions and of the United Kingdom and it is hereby affirmed that in no event will Northern Ireland or any part thereof cease to be part of His Majesty's Dominions and of the United Kingdom without consent of the Parliament of Northern Ireland.[13]

Welfare services, industrialization and I.R.A. violence were the prominent political issues in the Republic during the 1950s. Southern Irish politicians continued to urge an end to partition but discussions on that subject incited fewer passions each year. Elsewhere, conditions in the post-World War II era did effect changes in Northern Irish attitudes. Some Ulster nationalists came to understand that the wall of partition would not be blown away by the oratory of politicians in the South or destroyed by the courageous, albeit often mindless, efforts of I.R.A. activists. They also took a new look at the potential standard of living in a Northern Ireland supported by the British welfare state. Perhaps first-class citizenship was a more practical goal than a united Ireland. A few perceptive Unionist politicians also reevaluated the situation. The proportion of the Catholic population was increasing; someday Catholics would be a majority. Apartheid and oppression were not feasible as permanent policies. Civil rights struggles in the 1960s, particularly in the United States, had a significant impact on the mood of Northern Ireland.

Indeed, the 1960s began auspiciously and seemed to herald a new era of greater harmony and understanding in Ireland. An Anglo-Irish free trade agreement, reached in 1965, removed economic barriers that had hampered commerce between the Republic and the

Six Counties. The agreement was highlighted by a dramatic meeting between the Irish Republic's Prime Minister Sean Lemass and Northern Ireland's Prime Minister Terence O'Neill. Eamon de Valera was subsequently reelected president of the Irish Republic in 1966 and optimists speculated that the unification of the nation might be achieved during his term of office. But that was before the Civil Rights Association in Ulster (a nonpolitical, nondenominational organization which principally reflected the aspirations and frustrations of Northern Ireland's middle class) marched in August 1968 as part of a demonstration protesting poor housing in Dungannon. The movement spread and ugly confrontations ensued, leading to the battlegrounds of Londonderry and Belfast where British troops attempted to restrain both Catholic and Protestant militants from engaging in civil war.

The Northern Ireland Civil Rights Association, formally organized in 1967, was a coalition effort to achieve equal citizenship. Catholic middle-class moderates marched with Socialists, Republicans, Protestant liberals and university students, and they used the song of the American civil rights movement, "We Shall Overcome." Northern Ireland Prime Minister Terence O'Neill, partly at the urging of British Prime Minister Harold Wilson, made a few modest concessions which brought an immediate response from the fanatics of the Orange Lodges. Ian Paisley, the archenemy of popery, and William Craig, the leader of the Protestant Vanguard, led the counterattack. Caught between civil rights agitation and Orange fanaticism, O'Neill resigned. His successor, James Chichester-Clark, also promised changes but moved too slowly for Catholics and much too quickly for militant Orangemen. He too resigned and was succeeded by yet another moderate, Brian Faulkner. By this time, the days of moderation had passed. Orange extremists, the timidity of politicians, and the impatience of Catholic radicals—Socialist and Republican—combined to destroy the spirit and influence of the 1967 civil rights movement. The parliament at Stormont was also destroyed when Faulkner's Northern Irish government was suspended, in the summer of 1972, and replaced by direct rule from London after civil disorders threatened to thrust the Six Counties into a state of anarchy.[14]

What went wrong? Why did the sectarian hatreds of Ulster Protestants and Catholics plunge that province into chaos at the very time when many intelligent leaders in both the North and South of Ireland were inclined to place a higher premium on the quality of life than on the divisive issue of partition? Reduced to the simplest terms, the Protestant ascendancy had made little effort to assimilate the Catholic third of Ulster's population into the political and economic system. And that failure left two distinctly different cultures, diametrically opposed to one another and sharing the extremely limited confines of the same small state.

Northern Ireland has been a unique phenomenon in the British system. The Six Counties are part of the United Kingdom, sending 12 Members of Parliament to Westminster[*] but, until recently, the parliament at Stormont controlled local affairs.[15] Even under Ulster's new constitution, to have been implemented in 1974, the province would have an 80-seat assembly, which would be elected under a more equitable system of proportional representation. But from Northern Ireland's inception in 1920, to the suspension of Stormont in 1970, the Six Counties have remained as Ulster's first prime minister, Lord Craigavon, had said they should: a Protestant nation for a Protestant people. Even though Catholics constitute over one-third of the population, and have majorities in two counties, Fermanagh and Tyrone, and in Derry City, they are still second-class citizens in the Six Counties.

In housing, segregation is both politically imposed and self-imposed. Fear has induced Protestants in Belfast, for example, to seek the sanctuary of Protestant-inhabited areas like Shankill, and Catholics tend to settle with their coreligionists in districts like the Falls Road for the same reason. Segregated housing is perpetuated by the site location of new housing units. Such matters fall under the jurisdiction of local city councils, which are able thereby to apportion voting strengths through gerrymandering. Moreover, the local franchise was for years dependent upon ownership or tenancy of a dwelling of prescribed value. Those too poor to be householders were consequently disqualified from voting in local elections.[16] Even in areas where Catholics have a substantial majority—Derry City is just one example—Protestants dominate agencies of county and urban government. In the age of the welfare state, local governments select the recipients of jobs and public housing. Catholics, therefore, bear the biggest burden of unemployment and poverty, living in overcrowded, unsanitary tenements. Protestants dominate the police force, the Royal Irish Constabulary. Early in its existence, Northern Ireland established the B Specials (11,514 of them supplemented 2,867 regular police in 1936), an exclusively Protestant force which augmented the Constabulary. Although they were recently disbanded by the British government, the excesses of these legal vigilantes are still bitterly

---

[*]Neither Scotland nor Wales possesses any separate legislature for local affairs and both are represented at Westminster. The Isle of Man and the Channel Islands, by contrast, do have local legislatures but are without representation at Westminster. Only Northern Ireland has a local parliament and representatives at Westminster, a fact which makes it unique among the regions which comprise Great Britain.

remembered by Ulster nationalists. To Catholics, the B Specials were the Gestapo of a Protestant police state. And it was a police state. A Special Powers Act permitted authorities in Northern Ireland to arrest and imprison suspected Catholic nationalist subversives without ordinary legal procedures.[17]

Of course there are poor Protestants in Northern Ireland. A post-World War II decline in the shipbuilding and linen industries left Northern Ireland a depressed area living off the bounty of the British welfare state. Even agriculture suffered locally and in Britain from the industrial depression. But poor Protestants in Northern Ireland defy the rationale of socialist ideology. Despite the poverty and unemployment which they share with Catholics, Ulster Protestant workers and farmers follow the political leadership of the ultra-right Unionist party. The latter have used no-popery to control Six County politics and to avoid seriously confronting that region's severe social and economic problems, a burden made easier by the generosity of the British welfare state. Northern Irish politicians, from Craigavon to Paisley, have exploited the bigotry of the Protestant masses whose religious zeal is expressed in racist rhetoric. They believe Catholics to be an inferior species: lazy, superstitious, improvident, irresponsible and treacherous. Northern Irish Unionists accept as an article of faith that Catholics must be excluded from positions of power lest they destroy the existence of the Six Counties. There is, of course, justification for some of their apprehensions. Most Ulster Catholics are nationalists and they have traditionally regarded the partition of their country as an unholy bargain struck between Orangemen and British politicians.[18]

Catholic ghetto life in the Six Counties has produced a nationalism much more intense than that in Southern Ireland. Catholics never tire of recalling that they are descended from the ancient Gaelic stock that held Ulster for 1500 years and more until 1603; and that the Protestants must trace their ancestry to English and Scottish colonists who came to Ulster in the seventeenth century for the purpose of securing the province for England. Protestantism, the English language, a British life style, and allegiance to the British crown are part of the "colonial" tradition, just as Catholicism, the Irish language, an Irish way of life and an independent Ireland are in the "native" tradition. And these contentions are more real than rhetorical. Catholics do attend parochial schools which emphasize Irish history, culture and language; they play Gaelic football; and their Sunday night socials are frequently traditional folk-type dances. Protestants attend schools emphasizing British history and culture; they play soccer and rugby; and they dance to the rock music popular in Britain. The result has been the growth of two entirely alien and antagonistic groups existing side by side in a society made all the more precarious by economic depression and growing unemployment.[19]

Although Protestant alarmists interpreted the civil rights movement of the late 1960s as another subversive attempt by Catholics to achieve union with the Republic, the agitators were actually "more unionist than the Unionists" in that they sought "British standards" of administration. They asked the government to provide jobs, housing, better education, and greater suffrage for the Catholic minority, and marched and demonstrated to rally support for their cause. Two factors, not unusual in such a situation, undermined the efforts of the civil rights coalition: impatience on one side and fear on the other. Among Roman Catholics, and especially among the young, there was a strong feeling that they had waited too long and that the government must be forced to meet their complaints. Protestants were quickly drawn into ugly confrontations in defense of what they believed to be their imperiled institutions. It would, indeed, have taken time and skillful leadership to educate the Protestant masses to a new attitude of mind. They had been so long taught that the security of the state depended upon their solidarity and supremacy, and so deeply imbued with the idea that every Roman Catholic was an enemy, that they were easily driven to escalating the crisis at the urgings of demagogues.[20] Moreover, as some Catholics and civil rights activists despaired of any hope for legal redress, they turned to violence. And television brought a new dimension to the crisis. Formerly, when riots had occurred, news of them appeared only in the papers. Englishmen accustomed to viewing televised scenes of police brutality in places like Chicago were now horrified to see similar spectacles taking place in a part of the United Kingdom. Following the disorders of August 1969 public pressures forced the Labor government of Harold Wilson to intervene with British troops.[21]

Fear and impatience have taken a tragic toll in Northern Ireland as nearly 800 lives have been lost since the disorders began not many years ago. Even as British administrators for Ulster William Whitelaw sought to end the violence and restore peace with the help of 20,000 British troops garrisoned throughout the Six Counties, the London government pondered the jurisdictional compromises which might mollify both the Protestant and Catholic communities. In March 1973, London published a 34-page White Paper setting forth a firm policy to be supported by legislation in the British parliament. One of its objectives was to ensure a share of political power for the Catholic minority. Instead of the old 52-seat Stormont parliament, the paper proposed an 80-seat assembly, elected under a system of proportional representation. Turning aside the appeals of Protestant leaders, the British reserved the powers of security for the parliament in London. Westminster would also take over certain powers of taxation, the election laws, the administration of the courts, and the appointment of judges and magistrates—all previously the prerogative of the provincial government. Protestant Unionists were given the assurance again that they would not be absorbed into the Irish Republic unless they expressly consented to unification. Catholic nationalists were told that after the Assembly elections, a conference of delegates from Ulster and from the Irish Republic would meet to discuss future efforts at cooperation.

Reactions from various segments of the Six Counties included general welcome from most Catholic organizations and a toughening line from Protestant groups. British officials were relieved that the latter's statements promising resistance to the White Paper's proposals talked of electoral rather than violent methods. Both the I.R.A. and the militant Protestant Vanguard movement rejected the White Paper categorically, however, and spoke ominously about resolving matters through armed conflict. But the majority of Ulster's Protestants and Catholics desperately desire a respite from the violence and the physical force; advocates may find themselves isolated from the community and thereby rendered vulnerable or impotent.

Ulster's future remains uncertain. The British would welcome any opportunity to free themselves finally and completely from their Hibernian albatross. Considering the intensity of Six-County Protestant hostility to the government in Dublin, however, and the Irish Republic's concern for enforcing the dictates of Catholic morality, particularly with respect to legislation in the areas of divorce, abortion, birth control, and censorship, any immediate end to partition would only create another minority question and a constant threat of civil disorder in a 32-county nation. This is indeed unfortunate since unity between North and South, Catholic and Protestant, could promote greater liberty in Ireland. If the myths perpetuating religious and regional prejudices were discarded, a common effort could be made to solve the problems of poverty, unemployment, low agricultural production and emigration in all of Ireland. Unification would help Protestants and Catholics emancipate each other: Protestants from their fears and bigotry, Catholics from their parochialism. Indeed, the influx of a large Protestant minority would diminish the unwholesome influence of the Catholic Church on the government of the Republic.

Whether or not Ulster continues indefinitely as a semiautonomous part of the United Kingdom, or eventually joins the rest of Ireland in a completely new form of national government, as recently proposed by a prime minister of the Irish republic, 22 is of only secondary importance. What is immediately required of Catholics and Protestants in the Six Counties is a change in attitude and spirit. If a sufficient number of them are prepared to protect the civil rights of all citizens, they may learn that a common humanity is more important than religious creeds. Moreover, the United Kingdom and the Irish Republic's entry into the European Economic Community may very well lead to regional consolidations which have no reference to religious or political considerations. For Northern Ireland, the immediate resolution of its future affiliation need not be a crucial issue; the preservation of the principle of human rights, however, is all important and may determine the very survival of the community in the Six Counties.

NOTES

1. J. C. Beckett, "Northern Ireland," Journal of Contemporary History 6, no. 1 (1971): 121.
2. Two of the more standard references are J. C. Beckett, The Making of Modern Ireland: 1603-1923 (London: Faber and Faber, 1966); and T. W. Moody and F. X. Martin (eds.), The Course of Irish History (Cork: The Mercier Press, 1967).
3. Eric Strauss, Irish Nationalism and British Democracy (New York: Columbia University Press, 1951), p. 282.
4. T. W. Moody and J. C. Beckett (eds.), Ulster Since 1800 (London: British Broadcasting Corporation, 1957), p. 232.
5. The classic and most comprehensive study of this period is W. E. H. Lecky, History of Ireland in the Eighteenth Century, 5 Vols. (London, 1892).
6. See Stephen Gwynn, Henry Grattan and His Times (London, 1939).
7. Perhaps the most useful account of this episode is E. H. Stuart Jones, An Invasion That Failed: the French Expedition to Ireland, 1796 (Oxford: Oxford University Press, 1950).
8. An excellent account of the Orange Order is Hereward Senior, Orangeism in Ireland and Britain, 1795-1836 (Toronto: University of Toronto, 1966).
9. Lawrence J. McCaffrey, "The Catholic Minority in the North," in Divided Ireland: The Roots of the Conflict, ed. Francis W. O'Brien (Rockford, Illinois: Rockford College Press, 1971), p. 49.
10. George Dangerfield, The Strange Death of Liberal England (New York: Capricorn Books, 1961), pp. 71-138.
11. Charles L. Mowat, Britain Between the Wars, 1918-1940 (New York: Methuen & Co., 1968), pp. 106-08.
12. Strauss, op. cit., pp. 286-87.
13. Richard Rose, "The Dynamics of a Divided Regime," Government and Opposition 5, no. 2 (Spring, 1970): 174-75.
14. McCaffrey, op. cit., p. 53.

15. C. E. B. Brett, "The Lessons of Devolution in Northern Ireland," The Political Quarterly 41, no. 3 (July-September, 1970): 261.

16. Mary Bromage, "Ireland's Unfinished Revolution," The South Atlantic Quarterly 71, no. 1 (Winter, 1972): 25-26.

17. Cornelius O'Leary, "The Northern Ireland Crisis and Its Observers," The Political Quarterly 42, no. 3 (July-September, 1971): 256.

18. McCaffery, op. cit., p. 51.

19. Thomas E. Hachey, ed., The Problem of Partition: Peril to World Peace (Chicago: Rand McNally, 1972), pp. 38-39.

20. Beckett, op. cit., p. 133.

21. John Kane, "Civil Rights in Northern Ireland," The Review of Politics 33, no. 1 (January, 1971): 75.

22. John Lynch, "The Anglo-Irish Problem," Foreign Affairs 50, no. 4 (July, 1972): 614-15.

CHAPTER

2

DIVIDED BERLIN: ONE PAST AND THREE FUTURES
Richard L. Merritt

INTRODUCTION

Students of political integration have by now built up a sizeable repertory of case studies in which separate political systems ultimately did (or did not) integrate into a single larger system with centralized decision making, patterns of communication, symbols, political habits, and the like. A subset of these case studies comprises areas that once operated as single systems but, for one reason or another, broke up into several autonomous parts. In a limited sense, non-Soviet Europe acted as a single system before the events of World War II and its aftermath tore it asunder. Similarly, the postwar years have seen the division of countries or areas such as Germany, Korea, Indochina, India, and Palestine—in most cases, areas that had previously enjoyed strong intrasystemic ties and fairly sharp discontinuities with the outside. Another such case, in which even more intensive intrasystemic ties were broken, is the city of Berlin.

Postwar developments in Berlin have much to tell us about political integration and disintegration. Before 1945, Berlin was a unified community in its political structures and processes, economic and social infrastructures, and communication networks. Berlin was also the core area for Germany as a whole. Military occupation and

---

Reprinted with the kind permission of the Journal of Peace Research, Vol. 9 (Oslo: International Peace Research Institute, 1972).

the deepening cold war broke it into two cities, formally by 1948 and physically some 13 years later. Arrangements negotiated in 1971-72, although possibly easing access between East and West Berlin, will by no means put the Humpty Dumpty-like divided community back together again. In other regards, Berlin bears less resemblance to other divided polities, such as Korea. Prewar Berlin, as a city, was not autonomous: it was an integral part of a much larger political system, namely Germany. Nor had sharp political and cultural differences given rise to centuries of intrasystemic conflict, as was true with Europe. Postwar developments in the city nonetheless have much to tell us about integration and disintegration of mutually hostile political systems.

THE DIVISION OF GREATER BERLIN

Greater Berlin, one of the world's largest cities spatially and boasting almost 4.5 million inhabitants in 1943, suffered three successive waves of disruption during the next half-decade. The first came with aerial bombardments and, in April 1945 when the Red Army stormed the city, savage streetfighting. It reduced greater parts of the city to piles of rubble. The US Strategic Bombing Survey, for instance, estimated that 42 percent of Berlin's 1.5 million dwelling units were completely destroyed, and another 31 percent damaged to a lesser or greater extent; German sources estimated that they removed 98 million cubic yards of rubble from the city. (Nahm 1967, pp. 5-6, 74-77) Evacuations reduced its population by a third from the 1943 peak. The destruction also crippled Berlin's communication and transportation facilities no less than its capacity to provide such normal municipal services as electricity, gas, water, and sewage removal. The bombing and streetfighting nonetheless had a random effect as far as the eastern and western halves of the city were concerned. East Berlin, that is, the Soviet-occupied sector, lost 24 percent of its 1939 population and 22.9 percent of its industrial capacity, the three western sectors 27 percent of their population and 23.5 percent of their industrial capacity. East Berlin, with 37 percent of 1943 Berlin's dwelling units, accounted for 26 percent of the bombing losses during the next two years and 40 percent of the rubble. (Nahm 1967, pp. 82-83; Stat. Landesamt Berlin 1951, p. 15)

The effects of the second disruptive wave were distributed less equitably. Berlin fell to the Red Army on 2 May 1945, but not until 1 July did the Western Allies take over their occupation sectors in the city. During these two months Soviet occupation authorities extensively dismantled the city's industrial capacity, shipping it off to the USSR as reparations.* Possibly because of the unsettled nature of the reparations agreements, possibly because of the critical importance to the Soviet Union of western Berlin's industry, possibly (as Western writers have charged) because of the realization that the Red Army would eventually have to yield the western sectors to U.S., British, and French contingents, possibly (as Eastern writers have charged) because of concern that the West would fail to live up to the tacit agreements on reparations—whatever the cause, the effect was that dismantling during these two months cost West Berlin twice as much of its total industrial capacity (with the loss estimated variously as between 53 and 67 percent) as East Berlin had suffered (25-33 percent). (Nahm 1967, pp. 79-83)

The third disruptive wave constituted the division of the city itself. Soon after Berlin's joint occupation by the four powers, cooperation broke down along East-West lines. (See Davison 1958; Keiderling & Stulz 1970, esp. pp. 150-201) The underlying issues were global in scope, but it was in Berlin that their practical effects were felt. They had to do with the provision of electricity and other municipal services; arrests and other forms of harassment; control over records and historical documents; and midnight confiscations of garbage cans, trucks, and building material. By March 1948 the four-power Kommandatura split. Three months later, after the Western currency reform and the Soviet currency reform in response, came the blockade of the Western sectors of Berlin and the West's counterblockade of those areas in Germany and Berlin under Soviet control. The processes of quasi-unified municipal government broke down in August 1948, to be replaced by separate governments in East and West Berlin. A Soviet-U.S. agreement in May 1949 ended the blockade and counterblockade. However, it failed to resolve the underlying issues spawned by the cold war, and left Berlin a divided city.

The division of Berlin's formal political processes encouraged with time the development of separate social systems. This did not come all at once. From the end of the blockade until August 1961, the border remained open for Berliners to cross from one side of the city to the other. Bit by bit, however, the rate of interaction dropped

---

*The enemies of Hitler's Third Reich had never really reached a final agreement on reparations. At Yalta the Big Three had agreed in principle on the demand for reparations, and specific sums, such as Stalin's proposal of $20 billion, had been bandied about; postwar agreements even specified how transfers were to be made. But in the final analysis, behavior regarding reparations was decentralized, with each occupying power pursuing somewhat different policies in its own zone. See Kuklick 1972.

off. This can be seen in such diverse ways as the flow of visitors to the theater, knowledge about what was happening in the other part of the city, membership in joint organizations, and the flow of mail and other communications. Simultaneously, each side of the city began to develop infrastructural patterns that added physical dimensions to the border between East and West (Merritt 1973). This can be seen in traffic patterns, the development of highways, construction, and shifts of population. The construction in August 1961 of a wall between East and West Berlin merely put a seal of permanency upon processes already well under way.

The ensuing decade saw two cities living apart from each other. Residents of the one were not permitted to visit the other (except East Berlin pensioners; a few hundred residents in the one city who worked in the other; and, until 1966, West Berliners who could visit East Berlin on certain holidays, and, later, only in cases of family emergency). There were no telephone connections for public use. And even those organizations, such as the Evangelical Church in Germany, which maintained formal unity throughout the whole of Berlin, were ultimately forced to recognize the new boundaries and reorganize themselves separately. Only occasionally and through intermediaries—most notably the communications media, but also West Germans, who, unlike West Berliners, were permitted to visit East Berlin—could residents and officials in one city find out what was happening in the other. Cleared of ideological trappings, charges, and countercharges, what the world witnessed between 1945 and 1970 was the division of a previously integrated political community. And what is remarkable for students of political integration is that neither intense personal and cultural ties nor formal unity among numerous organizations could halt this process of disintegration.

The chance for a new relationship between East and West Berlin has developed only since late 1969. After Willy Brandt's accession to the chancellorship, West Germany undertook a new policy toward the East that quickly met a receptive response. Brandt met twice in early 1970 with the German Democratic Republic's premier, Willi Stoph—acts that constituted de facto if not de jure recognition of the GDR—and by the end of the year had signed treaties with both the Soviet Union and Poland that aimed at detente in central Europe. Brandt also encouraged the former allies of World War II to work toward a settlement of the Berlin issue that would look toward the future rather than dwell upon past resentments and juridical claims. This Berlin settlement, signed in September 1971, in turn set the stage for direct negotiations between East and West Germans on plans to implement the arrangements outlined by the four powers. Since all these agreements were tied intimately together, any significant misstep on the part of any of the signators could have wrecked the structure

DIVIDED BERLIN: ONE PAST AND THREE FUTURES 21

for detente. Bitter debate and frantic maneuvering notwithstanding, the West German Bundestag ratified the eastern treaties in spring 1972, and formal four-power accession to the Berlin accords followed soon thereafter.

The new climate soon produced payoffs for Berliners. For one thing, authorities in East and West agreed to the installation of telephone lines to connect the two cities. For another, East Berlin granted visitors' permits over Easter 1972 to West Berliners, most of whom had not been permitted to visit East Berlin in six years. Meanwhile agreements have been reached on access routes between West Berlin and the Federal Republic, regularized procedures for frequent visits by West Berliners to East Berlin, improved communication facilities, and cessation of some activities in West Berlin (such as meetings of the Bundestag in the city) that the GDR considered provocative. And above all there is the possibility that the complex of contractual relationships will ease the cold war tensions that have surrounded the city since 1945.

Viewed in systemic terms, the developments that I have described comprise one form of political disintegration. The process was not unlike that which occurs when a cell divides: an immense amount of energy was consumed when the nucleus split, but ultimately the components of the original unit regrouped themselves around the new nuclei. Similarly, as in the case of the cell, this form of disaggregation did not necessarily produce decay. Indeed, if we were inclined to argue along with Arnold J. Toynbee, we could even regard the traumatic split as a challenge that could elicit a creative response. What we may have missed in concentrating upon the demise through disaggregation of the pre-1945 political system of Berlin, however, is the fact that a new kind of total system with East and West Berlin as separate components has emerged. This recognition would lead us to ask what the political scenarios might be for the future development of this new political system.

THE FUTURE OF DIVIDED BERLIN

Several variables are important in trying to assess the future development of the two cities in the total system comprising Berlin: the ultimate disposition of the contractual arrangements that are still being worked out; relationships between East Berlin and the GDR on the one hand and, on the other, between West Berlin and the Federal Republic of Germany; intrasystemic change, particularly in West Berlin; exogenous variables such as relations between the United States and the Soviet Union, the FRG and its Common Market neighbors, and the GDR and its Warsaw Pact associates; and, not least, the attitudes and behavior of Berliners and Germans alike. At this stage I shall not discuss these in terms of independent and dependent variables, or even as a basis for empirical propositions, but rather in the framework of alternative scenarios for Berlin's future as a single political system.

The Cold War Renewed

One scenario, at this point rather improbable although certainly possible, would result from the failure by any party to implement the eastern treaties and Berlin accords in good faith. This could occur in a number of ways. It is conceivable that relaxed tensions might lead to a reduction of the U.S. presence in Western Europe, and that the Soviet Union would seize upon this opportunity to extend its own sphere of influence. It is also conceivable that West Germany would take advantage of a partial Soviet withdrawal to initiate a new diplomatic offensive aimed at isolating and eventually incorporating the GDR. Still another possibility would be an attempt by the United States to apply pressure on the Soviet Union in some future dispute by bolstering its troop strength in Europe. Incipient conflict with one or more of its allies could lead any of the major powers to see increasing tension in central Europe as a device for directing attention away from and defusing the dispute. Or East Germany might impose a partial or full blockade on West Berlin. Any such self-serving behavior could well nullify positive benefits accruing from the new status quo.

In any of these eventualities, Berlin might revert to the hotbox that it was for more than two decades. West Berlin would once again become the home of two million people anxious about their political future, a center of propaganda aimed at East Berlin and the GDR, and a symbol of the West's "steadfastness" and determination to protect "free" peoples from "totalitarian" pressures. Political insecurity would create increased tension within West Berlin that might push the municipal government toward greater measures of control. But such a situation might also carry some advantages for the city. Being in the spotlight once again might increase the level of federal assistance to the city, bring more tourists, and give its residents a renewed sense of having a special "mission" in world politics. Tension and perceived threats from outside their city's borders have more than once served an integrative function for West Berliners, both in increasing the ties of community within the island city itself and in expanding its ties with West Germany.

Renewed tension could also serve some policy aims in the East. The possibility of resurgent militarism in West Germany has been frequently used by the Soviet Union as a means for holding together the Warsaw Pact nations. It was an impending threat of West German intervention, for instance, that Soviet statements gave as a primary reason for their own intervention in August 1968 into Czechoslovakia. Similarly, the GDR has upon the occasion of severe domestic difficulties put the blame directly upon destructive meddling from West Berlin—such as in June 1953, when a construction workers' strike in East Berlin quickly spread to other cities in the GDR; or in August 1961, when the GDR constructed a wall between East and West Berlin.* The East German government has spent considerable sums in recent years to rebuild its capital city of Berlin as a counterdisplay to the glittering brilliance that is West Berlin. Renewed cold war tension might enhance the significance of such policies aimed at demonstrating socialist accomplishments; and, in this process, East Berliners could only benefit from new expenditures. By the same token, however, a tighter atmosphere in central Europe could lead the Soviet Union to assert more strongly its occupation rights in East Berlin, thereby retarding the city's integration into the GDR.

The cold-war system had a built-in stability of a short-run variety. Each side could utilize the threat ostensibly posed by the other as a basis for policies strengthening its own control mechanisms; and each could count on the other to deliver at appropriate intervals behavioral or verbal "evidence" to justify the perception of threat. This situation provided a certain security for all parties—by assuring the major powers that their satellites could not nor indeed would even be inclined to defect to the other side, and by assuring the smaller states of support in the event of any attack from the outside. Gray areas of cooperation or overlap between the two blocs were kept at a

---

*Otto Grotewohl, Minister President of the GDR, stated in July 1953 that the strikes of the previous month had encompassed 300,000 workers (or 5.5 percent of the total work force, excluding apprentices) in 272 towns; Western estimates are 375,000 workers (6.8 percent) in 274 towns. See Baring 1972, p. 52. Baring rejects subsequent Western claims that it was a popular uprising, and Eastern claims that Western agents provocateurs initiated it (although he allows [p. 88] that there were "isolated acts by West Berliners which were clearly premeditated" and that "it seems highly probable [my emphasis] that, once the disturbances had broken out in the eastern sector, the numerous western secret service organizations operating from Berlin will have done their utmost to bring their influence to bear"). See also Keiderling & Stulz 1970, pp. 311-16, 463-86.

minimum. The emphasis on control was nonetheless expensive. It cost large sums to maintain extensive military establishments, reduced the possibility of mutually profitable trade and other transactions, and, in particular, forced the parties to structure intrasystemic processes to sustain what approached Harold D. Lasswell's "garrison state." Even so, the system was stable only so long as neither side overstepped the line between mutual recriminations and mutually destructive hostility.

It is unquestionably possible to recreate in the 1970s the cold war system of the 1950s, and the degree of short-run stability and costs may be of the same order of magnitude as before. But in one regard the renewed cold war would be more intense and perhaps more dangerous than in years past: the frustrations of unfulfilled hopes aroused by the eastern treaties and Berlin accords of 1970-72 may well enhance the brittleness characterizing the system. For Berlin this would surely mean further steps toward distinctiveness. For West Berlin it would also mean enhanced dependence upon the FRG, and decreased possibilities for autonomous, creative development. And the prospects for long-run stability would be no better than before.

West Berlin Atrophied

In contrast to the cold-war system of symbiotic relationships shored up by negative supports is another possible development that appears equally improbable. The successful implementation of the contractual arrangements of 1970-72, while encouraging greater integration of East Berlin into the GDR, could also lead to West Berlin's atrophy within an environment of rapidly expanding economic and political development in the East. The Berlin accords, even if carried out with good will by all parties, can stabilize West Berlin's situation without allowing for adequate kinds of growth. The very diminution of tension that might ease life for West Berliners, for instance, could also make the city less visible to the West German population, which has poured large sums into West Berlin to maintain its economy. And the reduced presence of the Federal Republic in West Berlin called for in the Berlin accords could lead to some loss of jobs and work contracts.

Such events would in all probability accelerate trends in evidence for some years now. Young people seeking high-level careers in business and politics have been increasingly disinclined to see the island city as the most important area for their own futures. Indeed, the city has had to undertake extensive recruiting campaigns in West Germany to bring young workers to the city, and the federal government has cooperated in providing financial benefits (such as low taxes) for those who remain in or move to West Berlin. Recent estimates suggest that, if current rates of migration hold constant, the city will be able to hold its own during the next decade with respect to the number of workers and the overall age distribution of the population. If migration to Berlin slows down, however, then by 1980 the city will have a population vastly overaged relative to the inhabitants of the FRG.[1] This will cause an increase in West Berlin's social welfare budget, requiring even greater assistance from the Federal Republic.

All these developments in turn would weaken West Berlin's industrial base. Firms will be more inclined to tie themselves closely to the manufacturing and distribution network of the FRG, seeing West Berlin more in marketing than producing terms. Maintaining the economy of the city will require a search for possibilities in the service sector. The most likely of these (particularly given the curren problems faced by universities and research institutes in West Berlin) lies in tourism. But, again, the development of a larger tourist industry in West Berlin, with or without support from the federal and municipal governments, would force the city's population to restructure its own life style. Many citizens may prefer to leave West Berlin than to stay and watch that happen.

This scenario, then, foresees a downward spiraling of the quality of life in West Berlin. Trends in population composition, aging, economic patterns, and support requirements would be mutually reinforcing in leading toward a depressed and depopulated city. Such a development constitutes a special form of social and political decay: it is not that the West Berlin system would disintegrate and disappear completely, but rather that it would be forced to reorganize itself at another level of activity. Would this be catastrophic? Certainly not, particularly in relation to such possible consequences of continued tension as the outbreak of war over Berlin. But it would still have definite implications for the future development of divided Berlin's political system.

The outcome most easily envisioned would be a continuation of ties between West Berlin and the Federal Republic. Although of continued historic, symbolic, and cultural significance, the city would move even more to the periphery of West German life. Its economy would be precarious indeed. Not only would it be subject to normal economic exigencies—that is, expenditures for culture and tourism vary directly with a society's wealth—but it would also face the possibility that partisan considerations would force the government to curtail its subsidization of West Berlin. A gap might emerge between the glitter of the city's cultural centers and its more drab and somewhat depopulated residential areas. And in any event the attractiveness of East Berlin would continue to grow, raising the question of whether or not the FRG was prepared to subsidize visits to Berlin if the visitors were to flow in large numbers to socialist East Berlin to spend their tourist money. In such circumstances, we might expect West Germany to neglect West Berlin even more, thereby contributing to the dreary downward spiral.

It is also possible, however, to envision circumstances in which the FRG would be willing to relinquish its claim to West Berlin. The deteriorating conditions of the city, and the realization that only massive financial and political measures could restore it to its former brilliance, could well lead to despair. One response by West Germany to this sense of despair could be to blame the entire mess on the Western Allies who, according to wartime agreements and the Berlin accords of September 1971, continue to bear the major responsibility for the city's political future, and to wash its hands of the Berlin problem once for all. (Indeed, it might even be cheaper to evacuate West Berlin's 2.2 million residents to the FRG than to undertake any substantial salvage program in the city itself!) Such a decision would of course be fraught with implications for West Germany's relations with its EEC and NATO allies. And at the very least, regardless of whether or not the city ended up depopulated and abandoned, the United States, Great Britain, and France would hold an embarrassing hot potato in their hands.

Alternatively, with the acquiescence of these allies, West Germany might permit West Berlin to drift gradually into the GDR's orbit.* This could stem from a succession of purely practical decisions: West Berlin firms, for instance, might begin producing more for the East German market: this would lead the West Berlin economy more generally to attune itself to conditions prevailing in the GDR; and sooner or later some form of economic integration, such as a customs and payments union, would result. Or else West Germany could enter into explicit political deals with the GDR, exchanging a measure of control over West Berlin for something it wants, such as guaranteed free access between East and West Germany or increased trade. Unforeseen future shifts in the political complexions of the FRG and GDR could even lead West Berliners to push toward some degree of political integration within the latter. In any of these cases we might expect increased transactions between the two cities called Berlin, and a partial merger of their political processes and fates. Ultimately, with the tacit if not explicit consent of the West, the GDR and East Berlin might end the city's division by absorbing West Berlin.

---

*This may have been the scenario envisioned by Nikita S. Khrushchev when he proposed in November 1958 that West Berlin be turned into a "free city."

SISTER CITIES IN SEPARATE COUNTRIES

A more probable scenario is one projecting less extreme developments than the renewal of the cold war tensions or the "disappearance" of West Berlin. It rests upon the general acceptance of the eastern treaties and Berlin accords, and upon their implementation in good faith. It also rests upon the assumption that the Federal Republic is sufficiently desirous of maintaining its ties to West Berlin that it will continue its economic and political support. Finally, it assumes that West Berliners themselves treat the new status quo as a platform on which to build rather than a cause for despair. Each of these assumptions, I would argue on the basis of previous behavior and pronouncements by the concerned parties, is reasonable, although clearly not all will be fulfilled to the nth degree. Given their validity, however, what would be the likely consequences for the political system of divided Berlin?

Drive Toward Self-Sufficiency

In the political realm we cannot expect rapid steps toward rapprochement between East and West Berlin. First of all, the political division of the city occurred a quarter century ago. There has been little interaction between the two municipal governments since then. When their agents get together, they meet as representatives of foreign countries—common language and aspects of common culture notwithstanding. (See Carter 1969) This was not always the case, of course. As late as the mid-1950s they could meet as old colleagues who had a common background in the sense of both training and professional concerns. But bit by bit the older men retired or were replaced by younger men more congenial to the political decision makers, and in some cases they, too, were forbidden to meet formally with their counterparts in the other city. The construction in August 1961 of the wall eliminated the chance for even informal contacts. More generally, close to a generation of civil servants and politicians in the two cities has grown up in a new reality of separation, living in political systems with different values, concerns, and communication networks. It would be utopian to expect an immediate meeting of minds in the event that possibilities for contact grow.

Second, the trauma that accompanied the division of the city produced a legacy of bitterness and distrust that will require considerable time to smooth over. The municipal electricity company (BEWAG) may serve as a case in point. (Merritt 1968) Due to wartime damage and postwar dismantling, the western sectors of occupied Berlin were almost totally reliant upon the electrical output of power plants in the Soviet sector. Soviet representatives to the four-power Kommandatura saw no need to use scarce resources augmenting the electricity-producing capacities of power plants in the west since, they argued, those in East Berlin could provide enough electricity for the entire city. The British decision, supported by the United States and France, to reconstruct a power plant in its sector despite the absence of unanimity for this move within the Kommandatura contributed to the breakdown in March 1948 of that body. A crucial aspect of the subsequent blockade of West Berlin was the withholding of electrical power produced by Soviet-sector plants, with the consequence that West Berliners had as little as two hours of electricity per day throughout the 1948-49 winter. It was not surprising, therefore, that BEWAG-West set itself the task of making West Berlin totally self-sufficient in the production of electrical power. Even today, two dozen years later, there is a refusal in decision-making circles of West Berlin ever again to become dependent upon electricity from eastern sources—however inexpensive it may be compared to that produced in West Berlin. In this and other areas of day-to-day life, then, it is improbable that the opening of even extensive East-West contacts in Berlin will initiate an era of significant interaction, not to speak of mutual interdependence.

Third, in a very real sense there is little need for broadgauged political interaction between East and West Berlin. In practically all but geographic respects the two cities are self-sufficient.* Each of course relies upon its national government in a large variety of ways, and the wartime allies continue to enjoy occupation rights in their own sectors of the city, but both East and West Berlin are virtually independent of each other. In fact, once the practical details left open in the four-power Berlin accords are resolved, there need seldom be an occasion for the two cities' political representatives to meet again.

Much the same situation holds for the economic realm. There has almost always been trade between East and West Berlin within the framework of the "interzonal" trade agreements, and both the absolute and relative amount of this trade has grown in recent years. But, again, East Berlin officials remember attempts by the FRG to use trade as a political lever, most notably in late 1960 when it broke

---

*The major exception is the sewage system. West Berlin, currently in the process of constructing sewage treatment plants, continues to send untreated sewage to the leaching fields of the GDR, in exchange for a yearly fee. By the mid-1970s West Berlin may be independent in this regard as well.

off trade relations in protest over new regulations governing highway traffic between the FRG and West Berlin. Similarly, West Berlin officials have repeatedly made it clear that they are disinterested in increasing east-west trade up to the point where decisions made in East Berlin can adversely affect the economic and political well-being of West Berliners.

In social terms, the years of separation have doubtless diminished the interpersonal bonds between the two populations. Surveys taken over the course of the last two decades reveal that ever fewer West Berliners report a great longing to visit relatives or friends in East Berlin; and if we can use the differential responses of various age groups as an indicator, this trend will continue into the future, probably at an accelerated rate. Other indicators, such as the distribution of space in the religious press (which until 1970 represented the last major social institution to remain undivided), reveal a similar decline in interests among West Berliners about what goes on in the East. Half of the adult West Berliners nonetheless express a continued desire to visit relatives or friends in East Berlin.[*]

Ironically, perhaps, it is precisely in this self-sufficiency that the greatest hope for interaction lies. So long as either East or West Berlin feels that the other city can co-opt, overpower (through financial or other means), or absorb it, its decision makers will be reluctant to enter into negotiations. By now the two have achieved parity of political status. The treaties of 1970-72 explicitly guarantee that the signators will not use force to alter the territorial status quo in central Europe, will accept the GDR and East Berlin as legitimate bargaining agents, and recognize West Berlin as part of the FRG. Given this equality of status in fact if not always in name, representatives of the two cities can explore areas of possible cooperation that do not entail the creation of dependencies.

Dismantling Psychological Barriers

More a hindrance to fruitful interaction than the fact that they live in vastly different economic and political systems are the walls of

---

[*] A survey of about 400 West Berliners conducted in mid-March 1971 by the Institut fur Demoskopie (in <u>Allensbacher Berichte</u> 1971), revealed that 36 percent received occasional visits by pensioned East Berlin relatives, and 50 percent had relatives, friends, or acquaintances in East Berlin who were not pensioned and whom the West Berlin respondents would like to have seen again.

hostility and distrust that separate East and West Berliners. These barriers, as noted earlier, developed with the split of the city in the late 1940s. Governmental actions at the time and later, speeches by public officials and prominent citizens alike, and reports in the mass media both reflected this mutual antagonism and burned it into Berliners' consciousness. The subsequent decline of opportunities for people in either city to visit and learn about life in the other contributed its share to an informational vacuum in which the partisan views distributed in each seemed plausible to its own citizens. Compared to such psychological barriers separating peoples, the wall on the boundary between East and West Berlin is virtually a trifle.

A starting point for improved relations between the two cities may lie, then, in the image of the other that each presents to its own people. Government spokesmen could declare a moratorium on propagandistic statements. It may be too much to expect right now that they will scrutinize their own belief systems to remove less conscious elements of bias, but at the very least they could discontinue overtly inflammatory comments. Sometime in the future each government might find it helpful to appoint a commission of scholars and public officials (possibly from both cities) to examine growing differences in terminology and semantics, with the aim of modifying some of the less overt irritants—statements or expressions that spokesmen for one government may not even know exasperate and antagonize the other.

The governments can make other symbolic changes as well. West Berlin, for instance, could easily rename one of its major east-west arteries, now called "Street of the 17th of June" to commemorate the 1953 strike of some construction workers in East Berlin. This street, which leads to the Brandenburg Gate on the boundary line and then becomes "Unter den Linden" in the East Berlin borough of Mitte, might well be called "Peace Avenue" or "Berlin Boulevard" to stress the new atmosphere of detente. For its part, the East Berlin government could divert a part of its resources (possibly supplemented by funds from West Germany) to rebuild some more traditional Berlin landmarks destroyed in World War II, such as the National Theater. To reconstruct the Protestant cathedral or other churches in Mitte would require negotiation with the Church; perhaps their most appropriate use would be as museums of German church history, under the control of a mixed commission of clerical and secular officials.

School curricula and textbooks can be revised in ways to reduce mutual recrimination and encourage a better understanding of the other city and its national government. Schoolbooks have long been used by nationalists to instill into their youth a highly differentiated set of in-group and out-group attitudes. One's own nation is painted in rich detail, its history suitably tinted to present an image of past perfection, and its characteristics and life style described as norms toward which other peoples should strive; portraits of other nations, particularly those toward which the nationalists are hostile, tend to be caricatures, replete with omissions and more or less subtle misrepresentations. These tendencies have been no less the case in East and West Berlin. (See Merritt 1970) What is needed are programs in the two cities (and in the GDR and FRG) like the International Schoolbook Institute in Braunschweig. Supported by funds from West Germany, the Council of Europe, and Unesco, the Institute convenes international meetings of experts, exchanges books and other information, and consults with official and private sources in an effort to eliminate inaccurate passages in history texts and modify those that are less than flattering to other peoples; its accomplishments include agreements with several Western European countries, most notably France and Great Britain, as well as more recently with Poland. (See Multhoff 1970; New York Times 22 Oct 1972) There is little expectation that the textbooks used by different peoples will ever be identical, nor is it clear that they should be. More important at present is the removal or modification of gross distortions that exacerbate already complex national boundaries and the communication discontinuities they represent.

The media can also play a role in reducing mutually antagonistic attitudes. News reports in one of the Berlins, when they focus at all upon the other, tend to concentrate upon such negative events as potato shortages and student disruptions. These are important aspects of the news, to be sure, and should not be glossed over. The point is rather that, with just a little bit of effort, the press or television could also find some positive events to record: charitable or humane acts by police officers, improvements in the delivery of medical care, recognition received by actors and others, or even the pleasure of visiting the other city's zoo. It would be helpful to monitor news and other reports through a "detente quotient," or ratio of positive to negative space allocated to the other city. Governments could then extend laws and operating principles—normal in treating one's own citizens but rarely granted to those of other nations—requiring media to retract erroneous statements (or face libel suits) and giving representatives of alternative viewpoints ample opportunity to present their ideas and interpretations.

Completely free mobility of persons across the Berlin or German boundaries, which might facilitate understanding (if not always mutual affection), remains for some time in the future. A combination of circumstances—particularly differential economic opportunities afforded by the two countries, but also the consequences of political difficulties inherent in shifting the basis of a population's existence from a "free enterprise" system to a "socialist" one—led a great many

Germans to migrate from the GDR to the FRG. Stopping this flow was the chief purpose of the wall constructed in August 1961 around West Berlin, the main channel through which these "deserters" or "refugees" (as they were variously termed in East and West) passed into the West. It is therefore understandable that, without adequate guarantees, the GDR is less than anxious to remove controls over movements of its citizens. The two German governments have to be sure taken steps to ease the access problem. Agreements that went into effect in October 1972 expanded the opportunities for GDR residents to visit the Federal Republic and West Berlin in the event of "family emergencies," permitted West Berliners to visit East Berlin and the GDR on a regular basis, and, through the provisions of a new GDR law, gave greater degrees of mobility to former GDR citizens now resident in the West.*
The basic problem, however, remains: completely free mobility between East and West Berlin is unlikely until the economic levels of the two areas are comparable; and even then only if the FRG and GDR are able to agree on questions of migration, including quotas and the extradition of "illegal" border-crossers. †

Coordinated Behavior

Such symbolic steps as textbook revision can set a tone conducive to more directly cooperative measures that are nonetheless short of joint institutions. Increased and diversified trade can benefit both Berlins—provided, of course, that it creates no dependencies, and does not make more permanent any existing inequalities in productive levels. The lack of farmlands in West Berlin, for instance, requires that the city import food for its two and a quarter million citizens. But any long-term arrangement in which West Berlin exchanges manufactured goods for foodstuffs from the GDR would doubtless be unacceptable

---

*GDR legislation, enacted on 16 October 1972, took away citizenship from any of its residents who left the GDR before 1 January 1972 in violation of its laws, but added that no criminal proceedings or prosecution would be undertaken against such persons. The effect was to permit former GDR citizens, now resident in the West, to return to the GDR for visits without fear of arrest. See Binder 1972.

†This problem is not unlike the issue of equality of status discussed earlier. If free access is truly a goal of the FRG, then it may make sense for it to contribute to the economic development of the GDR and to enact legislation controlling the influx of "illegal" migrants or "refugees" from the GDR.

to the latter, for it would not only emphasize the production lag in the GDR but also fail to help the GDR develop its own industrial capacity. A more appropriate arrangement might be explicitly three-cornered trade, with East Berlin and the GDR exporting foodstuffs to West Berlin and manufactured goods to the FRG, the FRG exporting a commensurate amount of foodstuffs and raw materials to the GDR, and both the FRG and West Berlin sending manufactured goods to the GDR in amounts equal to what the latter sends them.

A variety of exchanges is also feasible. A type that promises many advantages and practically no disadvantages to both sides is cultural exchange—provided that the type, amount, and quality are roughly equal. An invitation extended by one city to a theatrical group in the other, for instance, would enrich the cultural life of the former and constitute high tribute to the cultural niveau and accomplishments of the latter. Similarly, it should be possible to resume the intercity sports competition interrupted in 1961. Either city could open its hospital and pharmaceutical resources to citizens of the other—at first, perhaps, on a quid pro quo basis but later on the basis of need. Universities in East and West Berlin could delineate a framework facilitating exchanges of some faculty members and students—at first, no doubt, in technical areas such as optics and diagnostic medicine, but later in social medicine and even the social sciences. Government offices and quasi-official agencies such as physicians' associations can routinely send statistical and other unclassified technical reports to their counterparts in the other city. It might ultimately be possible to coordinate such diverse matters as highway construction and ecological control through the exchange of information.

All-Berlin Institutions

At all stages of the reconciliation process between East and West Berlin, but particularly at the later ones, joint committees of an ad hoc or permanent nature may be mutually advantageous. An all-Berlin film festival held under the auspices of a bilateral committee could attract even more worldwide attention than do the separate ones held each year in East and West Berlin. Joint international congresses of specialists or technicians are also conceivable; and scholars in some fields may be able to organize joint research projects. An all-Berlin mini-Olympics is also possible. All these enterprises, organized by ad hoc committees with the tacit or explicit sanction of the two governments, would entail very low political costs. If they proved successful, then both East and West Berliners would benefit, as would other participants in any international congresses or festivals, and they could serve as the basis for further and more extensive events. If they should be less successful, then it would be possible to end them without engendering great political crises—unless, of course, one government or the other should decide to seize upon the incident as a pretext for a broader political offensive.

Permanent functional committees can also pave the way to improved relations within Berlin. Since they share a common ecology, including the Spree River which flows through the hearts of East and West Berlin, they have a common interest in environmental control; an air or water pollution board in only one city will hardly be able to achieve its maximal goals. Consultation between representatives of both cities' environmental control boards might well lead to a permanent liaison office and ultimately, although certainly not in the immediate future, a single agency with jurisdiction throughout Berlin. Such liaison offices would also facilitate the provision of municipal services (electricity, gas, water, sewage disposal, transportation), highway and other aspects of city planning, and even the resolution of longstanding legal issues, such as property claims left over from World War II. In this respect, joint arbitration procedures could also clarify numerous nagging points of contention.

On a broader level, joint efforts may enhance the status of the two Berlins in their common political and economic environment. Regularized shuttle services between and perhaps even landing privileges in the two international airports in West Berlin and that in Schonefeld on the outskirts of East Berlin could again make the city a central node of the European transportation network rather than two terminal points of lesser importance. A world trade center, located somewhere on the boundary between East and West Berlin, could give manufacturers in each the opportunity to display their products on a continuing basis to the international marketing systems which the other represents. A "free trade zone" located in such a strategic position could turn the city into a highly significant entrepot of world trade.

All these are, to be sure, small steps, and I do not want to argue that their accomplishment would go far toward resolving either the major issues separating East and West Berlin or even their most important economic problems. Poorly conceived or executed measures could well reinforce residual distrust. Those that create dependencies or that are not based upon the principle of equality of status are likely to be dismissed out of hand. And, for the rest, the governments of the two cities must consider what might be called their cost-effectiveness: is either city likely to gain more by expanding the range and scope of contacts between East and West Berlin, or by concentrating more of its economic and political attention on relations with its national government? Successful efforts to build up east-west contacts in Berlin may nonetheless contribute toward creating a climate in which more significant issues can be tackled. And it is precisely the nature of this political climate that will determine the long-range future of Berlin.

THE LONG-RANGE FUTURE OF POST-DETENTE BERLIN

What is likely to come of the opportunities provided under the Berlin accords of 1970-72? Will a moderate level of east-west detente and increased access in fact encourage greater contacts, and will these in turn lead to a reconciliation of the two Berlins? It is possible to envision the eventual development of a network of social, political, and economic ties sufficiently compelling that the two cities would begin to merge again. In such a case, the intensity of day-to-day interaction would yield a Berlin that is more unified than the two Germanies. If UN protection could be substituted for that provided by the four World War II allies, who continue to exert their occupation rights in the city, then the new Greater Berlin would function as a neutralized free city. It might serve as a locus for incipient all-German or even all-European institutions.

However possible, it is still premature to entertain seriously such a forecast. First of all, it should be clear that no such development is likely without substantial, mutual satisfaction with progress on implementing the Berlin accords. Initial steps have moved surprisingly smoothly, given the level of hostility and vitriolic rhetoric that prevailed during the 1960s and earlier.' But, as the saying goes, one swallow does not make a summer. The two Germanies, not to speak of Nazi Germany's enemies during World War II, have some distance to go before we can speak casually of reconciliation.

Second, the idea of a neutralized free city goes directly against positions firmly held in the past in both the East and West. The GDR has long rejected the notion of yielding up East Berlin to some new Greater Berlin not under its direct control. West Berliners have been equally adamant in their refusal to accept the idea of the United Nations as a substitute for U.S., British, and French troops. In short, the level of tension in central Europe will have to be much lower than it is now before the GDR and FRG will voluntarily relinquish territory and people under their control in the interests of all-Berlin unity. And the desire for German reunification—not only the desire of the two Germanies for such a goal, but also that of other relevant states, such as France, Poland, the Soviet Union, and the United States—will have to be much stronger than it is now before Berlin can serve as a symbol not of the cold war that has separated them but rather of social, political, and economic ties that bind them together.

Finally, it is by no means clear that enhanced opportunities for east-west contacts in Berlin will produce anything resembling a drive toward merging the two cities. Consider, for example, interpersonal contacts. Arrangements completed in October 1972 permit West Berliners to visit East Berlin and the GDR for 30 days per year; and the East Berliners may visit the West in the event of family emergencies, such as serious illness or death. Doubtless, large number of Berliners will utilize this opportunity at the outset. It is doubtful, however, that a high rate of visiting will continue indefinitely. We might rather anticipate a resumption of the declining trend in evidence before the restrictions imposed in August 1961. Even more difficult to predict is how residents of one Berlin will respond to what they find awaiting them in the other. Some will renew ties of family and friendship, others will meet new people at the opera or pub, and still others will be sufficiently unsettled by the sense of foreignness they discover that the experience will be an outright painful one. Reintegration of the two peoples may thus be hindered more by the social drift of the past score and more years than by the political rift that caused it in the first place.

The emerging political system envisioned in this scenario, then, is not a reunified Berlin (or Germany). Far from it. The existence of two Berlins is likely to continue for a long time into the future. It is the clear-cut recognition of this fact by both Germanies, I have argued, that is a necessary precondition for a more realistic appraisal of inter-city relationships. Almost a generation of separation cannot cover up the communalities that link East and West Berlin their shared heritage of history and culture, the same physical environment, more than latent ties between the two populations, and the possibility of fruitful interaction in many regards. The years of separation superimposed upon these communalities has produced a mixed effect. On the one hand, they helped East Berlin decision makers to better organize the territory and population under their control into a self-sufficient political unit. On the other hand, however, the very artificiality of the separation was costly, both in terms of the personal anxieties and international tensions it produced, and in terms of losses stemming from the failure to adopt cooperative processes (such as recreation of a unified electrical power network) that would maximize the efficient utilization of resources.

Numerous areas of life begging for more cooperative processes do not endanger the principle of separate but equal status. Implementation of the Berlin accords of 1970-72 will permit enhanced ties of interaction for mutual benefit. I am not speaking here of unified districts or political decision-making processes. They will come, if at all, at a much later stage in any eventual rapprochement, and probably only after significant shifts in the structure of European and world politics as a whole. What is more likely is a series of small cooperative steps that will do little more than make the lives of Berliners more comfortable or less complicated. Such steps may result from overt behavior, such as joint projects or even permanent liaison offices, or else from tacit strategies of separate but coordinated behavior. To the extent that they prove successful, they may tie East and West Berlin together much as sister cities facing each other across more "normal" political borders or such natural barriers as rivers. To the extent that policy planners want detente in the Berlin area, it behooves them to search out not the grandiose schemes for reunification, but rather those areas of limited, low-risk, but cumulative cooperation between autonomous entities.

SUMMARY

Postwar developments in divided Berlin have much to tell us about political integration and disintegration. The city endured successive waves of wartime destruction, postwar dismantling, and, after 1948, political division. Structural division was made more permanent after 1961. Not until 1970-72 could the wartime allies and the two postwar Germanies work out contractual arrangements to regulate interaction between East and West Berlin. Despite cultural, geographic, and other affinities, the two cities have become and remain separate entities.

One possible but improbable future development is the failure of some party to fulfill the letter and spirit of these arrangements, leading to a renewal of cold-war tension. Another equally improbable scenario envisions the internal decay of West Berlin or its eventual abandonment by the Federal Republic, leading to its absorption by the German Democratic Republic. A more probable scenario sees East and West Berlin developing as sister cities in separate countries. This would necessitate a clear-cut recognition of both the two cities' autonomy from each other as well as the legitimacy of this status quo. Each could then work on matters of mutual interest without fearing a loss of control over its own fate.

NOTE

1. Statistisches Landesamt Berlin. <u>Berliner Statistik: Statistische Berichte</u>, A I 8 - 70 of 30 June 1971, "Vorausgeschatzte Bevolkerung und vorausgeschatzte Zahl der Erwerbspersonen in Berlin (West) 1970 bis 1980 nach Altersjahren (ohne Wanderungen)"; and A I 8 - 70 of 15 November 1971, "Vorausgeschatzte Bevolkerung in Berlin (West) 1970 bis 1980 (einschlicsslich Wanderungen)."

REFERENCES

Allensbacher Berichte 1971, No. 8.

Baring, A. M. 1972. Uprising in East Germany: June 17, 1953. Ithaca, N. Y.: Cornell University Press.

Binder, D. 1972. Accord ratified by 2 Germanies, New York Times, 18 October, p. 17.

Carter, F. T. C. 1969. The influence of political change on language in East Germany, Loughborough Journal of Social Studies no. 7, pp. 25-38.

Davison, W. P. 1958. The Berlin blockade: a study in cold war politics. Princeton, N. J.: Princeton University Press.

Keiderling, G. & P. Stulz 1970. Berlin 1945-1968: Zur Geschichte der Hauptstadt der DDR und der selbstandigen politischen Einheit Westberlin. Berlin (East): Dietz Verlag.

Kuklick, B. 1972. American policy and the division of Germany: the clash with Russia over reparations. Ithaca, N. Y.: Cornell University Press.

Merritt, R. L. 1968. Political division and municipal services in postwar Berlin. In Public Policy 17, ed. J. D. Montgomery and A. O. Hirschman. Cambridge, Mass.: Harvard University Press.

Merritt, R. L. 1970. Perspectives on history in divided Germany. In Public opinion and historians: interdisciplinary perspectives, ed. M. Small. Detroit: Wayne State University Press.

Merritt, R. L. 1973. Infrastructural changes in Berlin. Annals of the Association of American Geographers 63.

Multhoff, R. 1970. The work of the Brunswick International Schoolbook Institute in revising history textbooks. Western European Education 2: 71, 85.

Nahm, P. P. (ed.) 1967. Dokumente deutscher Kriegsschaden, Vol. IV/2: Berlin—Kriegs- und Nachkriegsschicksal der

Reichshauptstadt. Bonn: Bundesminister fur Vertriebene, Fluchtlinge und Kriegsgeschadigte.

New York Times, 22 October 1972. Poles and West Germans join to make their schoolbook history more objective, p. 25.

Statistisches Landesamt Berlin 1951. Berlin in Zahlen 1951. Berlin (West): Kulturbuch-Verlag GmbH.

Statistisches Landesamt Berlin 1971. Berliner Statistik: Statistische Berichte A I 8 - 70 (30 June) and A I 8 - 70 (15 November).

CHAPTER 3

SOCIALIZATION AND INTEGRATION STRATEGIES: THE CASE OF THE FEDERAL REPUBLIC OF GERMANY AND THE GERMAN DEMOCRATIC REPUBLIC

Arthur M. Hanhardt, Jr.

This chapter begins with the assumption that supportive political socialization patterns are important if reunification strategies for divided nations are to succeed. I shall examine this notion in the case of the Federal Republic of Germany (FRG) and the German Democratic Republic (GDR), knowing full well that my assumption is open to challenge. Indeed, last year, when we met in a similar panel, Henderson and Cho pointed out that in the case of Korea, unification and division are dependent upon international forces beyond the effective influence of domestic factors. Much the same holds for the Germanies. As C. L. Sulzberger recently noted in discussing Brandt's theory of a single German nation divided by ideology, ". . . reunification can come only when Europe itself drops or completely riddles existing political barriers, even if prevailing political labels remain on either side."[1] In other words a divided Europe must be overcome before reunification can come about.

That is also the argument of the government of the Federal Republic. As most recently stated by Chancellor Brandt, the prospects for reunification appear dim: "Without prejudice to the differing views on the national question as put on the record in the basic treaty, the Federal Government will treat the GDR as an independent, sovereign state and make corresponding arrangements with it. We know the differences in the social systems of the two German states. They divide us more than our divergent views on the nation."[2]

For its part, the government of the GDR is pursuing a policy of <u>Abgrenzung</u> (demarcation), which denies the existence of any single German "nation" and which seeks to differentiate as much as possible the GDR from the FRG. While minimizing contacts with the West, the GDR leadership is seeking to develop its socio-economic system

SOCIALIZATION AND INTEGRATION: GERMANY

on the model of an ideal socialist state. The GDR attitude was clearly stated by Erich Honecker shortly after he assumed the office of first secretary of the Socialist Unity Party (Sozialistische Einheitspartei Deutschlands [SED]) in 1971:

> When one speaks about the development of relations between the GDR and the FRG such development can rely only on the principles of peaceful coexistence between sovereign states with different social orders . . . . In this way and only in this way can things be judged so long as the FRG is an imperialist state. And if in the West anyone harbours the idea of 'swallowing' the GDR, of being able to liquidate our Socialist social system, it will be expedient to remind the gentlemen that the GDR, a stable Socialist state, is an inseparable part of the mighty Socialist community, that behind the GDR is the entire force of the Soviet Union and the united countries of Socialism.[3]

If, as their leaders contend, the Germanies have two very different social systems, then it can be presumed that distinct political cultures are and have been developing in East and West since the establishment of the two German states in 1949. An important aspect of the political culture concept is the manner and content of political socialization, ". . . the process whereby political attitudes and values are inculcated as children become adults and as adults are recruited into roles" in society.[4]

Returning to my opening assumption, I intend to look at some of the outcomes of the political socialization process in the FRG and GDR, and attempt to interpret these outcomes for their implications regarding reunification strategies. The data will be drawn from studies done on the educational systems of the FRG and GDR along with public opinion polls.[5]

At the end of World War II, each of the occupation zones formulated educational reform programs. In the West the most ambitious reeducation program was undertaken in the U.S. Zone. By and large, the American effort failed due to a lack of staff and initiative and an underestimation of the difficulty of inculcating democratic norms.[6] In the developing cold-war atmosphere, reeducation gave way to exchange programs and advisory relationships with the West Germans. Education for democracy in West Germany continued to receive important impulses from the United States and Western European countries.[7] And the degree to which norms and attitudes supportive of a democratic political system have become established in the FRG has been the subject of intensive social research.

In discussing political socialization through education in the FRG it is necessary to keep in mind that each _Land_ (State) government has control over its educational policies and programs. The federal government has only limited influence. For this reason there are large variations in quality and content of curricula among the various parts of the FRG. It is also important to realize that relatively little has changed in the formal structure of West German education since the late 1940s. Even though some alternate routes to university education have opened up in recent years for those who did not attend university preparatory schools, higher education tends to remain the preserve of the upper middle class in the FRG.[8]

What composite can be drawn of political socialization through the schools in the FRG? One of the persistent problems has been the gap between political theory and political practice, particularly as perceived by the young. Political knowledge has certainly increased among the young, partly because the civics curriculum has expanded. However, U.S. and West German investigators have shown that the content of political education tends to be formalistic and legal rather than participatory or functional, thus contributing to the disparity between theory and practice.[9] As young people mature their interest and knowledge about politics tend to increase. Yet opinion polls show that 63 percent of the 16-29 year old group sampled in the FRG were either not at all or not particularly interested in politics during the mid-1960s.[10] At this time a number of rather gloomy studies of German youth were published, among them one that concluded that "they are ripe for a new fascism."[11]

Cross-national studies have shown that while West German youth rank higher than English and American in terms of faith in their government's responsiveness, a disturbing (and comparatively greater) percentage seem quick to sacrifice civil liberties and to suppress rights of dissent. A 1969 study by A. N. Oppenheim included the following results under the category of "support for civil liberties":[12]

	England	FRG	Sweden	United States
Citizens must always be free to criticize the government	.422	.383	.396	.688
People who disagree with the government should be allowed to meet and hold public protests	.379	.234	.383	.370

Judith Gallatin and Joseph Adelson came to much the same conclusion when studying comparative populations of West German, British and American adolescents. They inferred a "slightly greater willingness to acquiesce to potentially restrictive laws," which "seem[s] to reveal a somewhat childlike approach to government, an orientation that we and others have elsewhere characterized as 'authoritarian submissive.'"[13] Indicative of the difficulties that research in this area presents is Gallatin and Adelson's inability "to explain why fully half of our German subjects advocated making freedom of speech laws permanent."[14]

Clear results are not to be expected from the literature being reviewed here. Yet there are tendencies, such as in Hans Weiler's finding that dissent toleration increases directly with level of school education,[15] which lead to generally more optimistic conclusions than those of the mid-1960s regarding political socialization consistent with and supportive of the political system of the FRG.[16]

In contrast to the FRG, the goals of political socialization in the GDR are centrally determined by the state. One of the principal aims of the educational system of the GDR is to inculcate the values and norms of the socialist personality in pupils and students. While an exact definition of the socialist personality is not possible, a representative source described it as follows: "The socialist personality is the embodiment of the unity of the theoretical and the practical. It is characterized by the inseparable unity of the scientific world view of dialectical materialism, socialist morality, and social-political action in the construction and strengthening of socialist society."[17] And Walter Friedrich, the leading social psychologist working in the area of adolescence and youth in the GDR, has written that in developing their socialist personalities, it is very difficult to give substantive content to definitions of this kind, the concept of a socialist personality has figured prominently in the literature long enough to be useful as an indicator of what the GDR education system is supposed to achieve. My thesis here is that the closer the socialist personality comes to realization in the GDR, the further apart the two German political cultures will have been moved—in part by the political socialization process. This thesis will be illustrated in a discussion of recent examples of empirical research done in the GDR that might facilitate an assessment of the extent to which the goal has been achieved.

The development of the GDR educational system can only be sketched here. Radical reforms of the 1945-49 period readied the educational system for the transition to the polytechnical school, which came about in 1958 and 1959. This was a pivotal change in the system, and moved it toward closer integration with the economic system. It was a conscious attempt to implement a unification of theory and practice, along with other precepts of the socialist personality. In tune with dialectical materialism and the Marxist image of man, the changes were aimed at "training . . . children to love work and the working man."[18] In the words of the law establishing the polytechnical schools:

Polytechnical training and education is fundamental and a component of instruction in all school grades. Relative to the children's age, instruction will be combined with socially useful activity, or related to productive labor. Central to polytechnical instruction in the lower grades will be industrial arts and from the seventh grade on, instruction in socialist production.[19]

By the mid-1960s, following the introduction of the New Economic System in the GDR, enough experience had been gathered in the polytechnical schools to revise the program. The 1965 "Law on the Integrated Socialist Educational System" stated that "the goal of the integrated socialist educational system is a high level of education for all the people; the education and training of well rounded and harmonious socialist personalities who, while consciously structuring society, lead a fulfilled, happy, and dignified life."[20] With this law and the later introduction of new lesson plans in Staatsbuergerkunde (Civics), greater emphasis was placed on social studies in the curriculum and concern with the inculcation of the socialist personality was intensified. This emphasis emerges clearly from a survey of curricular changes introduced between 1966 and 1972. During this period, about 38 percent of the instructional time in the polytechnical school was taken up with social studies, German, and art, while 11.4 percent was devoted to polytechnical instruction and 32.1 percent to mathematics and natural sciences. The balance of the curriculum consisted of foreign languages (10.8 percent) and physical education (7.6 percent).[21]

An important supportive factor in the achievement of socialist personalities is the satisfaction that young people express concerning the environment providing the socialization experience. In 1962 and 1964, Friedrich noted a dissatisfaction level of 10 and 9 percent respectively with regard to the family setting. A greater degree of dissatisfaction emerges from Friedrich's findings concerning student assessments of their teachers. Those who would choose to have their classes conducted differently from their teachers' practices ranged from 9 percent of the eighth graders to 23 percent of the twelfth graders in the elite extended high schools.[22] Effective interpretation of these findings is limited for lack of comparative time series data. Nonetheless this study is one of the few that deals with the dissatisfaction factor.

How effective has the ten-year polytechnical school been in shaping the character of pupils to conform to the mold of the socialist personality? No firm answer to that question can be given at this point, or at least no firm answer that is based on survey or other research materials employing a measure of achievement in terms of the sought-for ideal; some approximations of the state of the socialist personality can be made from the results of research done in the GDR by social psychologists, educationalists, and other social scientists. These studies, in addition to personal observations made in the GDR, should facilitate an assessment of the impact of education in the development of socialist personalities.

Certainly one of the basic aspects of any definition of the socialist personality is an interest in politics. Although interest and knowledge are not in themselves indicators of commitment or of any particular internalization of values and norms, they are an essential element if the program of political education is to have an impact. Walter Friedrich has emphasized the importance of group factors in sparking political interest. Teacher competence, quality of the class collective, and group norms are among the factors Friedrich has discussed.[23]

A study by Mueller and Schedlich shows the kind of variation in political interest that can be found among schools and classes in the GDR.[24] Among the questions asked of students in the extended high school (which leads directly to university matriculation) one inquired: "Do you follow political events with (a) Great interest, (b) Middling interest, (c) Weak interest, or (d) Virtually no interest?" The results are shown in Table 8.1.

The table is interesting for at least two reasons. First is the difference in type of school and the corresponding interest in political events. The A-type school is the modern language and the B-type the mathematical-natural science extended high school, which prepares the best students for higher education. Among the natural science

TABLE 4

Political Interest Among GDR Schools and Classes
(in percent)

	Great Interest	Middling Interest	Weak Interest	Virtually No Interest
Eighth grade, A-type	61	35	4	0
Eighth grade, B-type	22	45	11	22
Twelfth grade, A-type	70	26	4	0
Twelfth grade, B-type	18	73	9	0

Source: Adolf Kossakowski, Zur Psychologie der Schuljugend (Berlin: Volk und Wissen, 1969), pp. 150-51.

TABLE 5

Concept of Freedom Among GDR Youth
(in percent)

	12-year-olds	14-year-olds
Freedom is understanding the necessary	0	0
Analogous response	58	40
Freedom is personal freedom	28	50
Unclear or indefinite response	14	10

Source: Rudolf Maerker, Jugend im anderen Teil Deutschlands (Munich: Juventa, 1969), p. 76.

students there is clearly less interest in political events than among their modern language colleagues. This could indicate that either the quality of ideological education is lower than in the B-type school or interest in political events is not encouraged by the curriculum. A second point of interest is the variation in interest shown by a comparison of the eighth grade responses to those of the twelfth. While the A-type shows an increase in interest, the B-type schools show a slight decline in interest in political events among those in the high interest category.

Research by Werner Hennig further substantiates the relative lack in importance of politics in the hierarchy of interests of the young. Interest in politics was found to be of only medium importance among 11- to 18-year-olds, being named by only 5 to 6 percent of those interviewed. In general, politics was found to be outside young people's main constellation of interests.[25]

It is hard to be conclusive in speculating on the reasons for these results, partly because there is no indication of the sizes of the samples or their distributions. However, Table 8.1 does indicate that there are significant variations in the extent to which students exhibit interest in political events in the GDR. This would further imply that there is some distance to go before the socialist personality is achieved. Such a conclusion is made more tenable by research carried out under the auspices of the Central Institute of Youth Research in Leipzig, which found an $r = .5$ correlation between interest in politics and pride in GDR citizenship among pupils.[26] If the extent of interest, and, by implication, pride in citizenship, is actually reduced in the high-interest category at the culmination of the education process for individuals in the natural sciences—precisely that class of students which, given the tenets of dialectical materialism and the precepts of the socialist personality, should exhibit the most marked increase—then it is difficult to avoid concluding that (1) not only is the educational process failing to adequately develop socialist personalities, but (2) it is actually moving away from the achievement of that goal.

In Table 8.2 we report the findings of Friedrich's research on GDR youth, tapping the content of political education. In a survey of 12- and 14-year-old pupils, Friedrich sought to determine how well those interviewed understood the Marxist-Leninist conception of freedom as "understanding the necessary" (Freiheit ist Einsicht in die Notwendigkeit).

The first response is the one taught in school. It would be the answer that the socialist personality would give to the question: "What is freedom?" Of primary interest, for present purposes, is the increase in those defining freedom as "personal freedom" in the older age group, since the expected direction of change would be toward the formally desired response. This suggests that in the mid-1960s there was a considerable amount left to be done in achieving one of the formal aspects of the socialist personality. Once again, it must be noted that the trend is apparently moving away from the stated goals of the educational system in the GDR.

Another noteworthy aspect of the socialization process in the GDR has to do with the self-image of the youth and their images of others. If socialization according to the desires of the political leadership is actually taking place, then the expectation would be that East German students would see themselves as resembling the images of the citizens of other socialist countries. This expectation was borne out in a study by Ulrike Siegel, who examined the national images of 431 students in the Leipzig area in 1964,[27] using a technique similar to that of Buchanan and Cantril in their UNESCO study of international stereotypes.[28] By having students apply a list of characteristics (hard-working, aggressive, intelligent, and so on) to the populations of various nations, Siegel found that the profile of the GDR self-image correlated highly with the profile of the students' image of the Soviets and the Cubans ($r = .945$ in each case). At the same time the students' image of the FRG correlated strongly with that of the United States ($r = .912$). The correlation between the GDR and the FRG images was $r = .768$. To the extent that these findings indicate growing distinctions and demarcations, this can be taken as an indicator of a reorientation in line with the ideological goal of "socialist solidarity," an international aspect of the socialist personality.

The research of Wolfgang Kessel underlines the desirability of having "committed" teachers to enhance the development of socialist personalities. Such teachers provide the unity of "idea" and "action" sought in the socialist personality and in the collective style of democratic centralism. In this regard, Jean Edward Smith has noted the frequency of SED party emblems on the lapels of teachers.[29] Although data are not available, it would appear from his observations (and mine at a teacher-training academy in Dresden) that care is taken to ensure that teachers set a political example for their pupils. One way of assuring this is to encourage party membership as a matter of principle.

The importance of proper examples was emphasized in the work of Friedrich and Schmidt on the effect of "prestige persons" on youth opinion. Fourteen- to 16-year-olds were surveyed on a variety of questions such as "Certainly the athletes of our Republic will win more gold medals in the 1968 Olympics than they did in 1964. What do you think?" Then an opinion was given by a prestige person such as a popular teacher or public official. Later the survey was administered again to find out how or if opinions had been influenced in the direction of the prestige person. The influence effect was found to be significant, especially among topic areas wherein attitudes and opinions were not already firmly established. Additionally there was an item "only in socialism is it possible for people to consciously form the life of society and to reach planned goals. What do you think?" Unfortunately the scale of positive-to-negative responses was not given in the research report. The authors did report that "a very large portion" of the students responded in the affirmative.[30]

On the other side of the desk, efforts have been made to harness the influence of peer groups in the socialization of students to values and attitudes consistent with the conception of the socialist personality. The most influential educational philosophy being applied is that of the Soviet pedagogue A. S. Makarenko. Urie Bronfenbrenner recently published a study describing peer group socialization in the United States and the U.S.S.R.[31] My impression of the GDR is that its atmosphere is similar to that of the Soviet Union when it comes to organized peer groups in the educational process.

The influence of peer group pressure to conform can be seen in the Jugendweihe, the ceremony in which youths turning 14 are brought into the community of citizenship. A majority of youths participating in the Jugendweihe, according to one study, stated they did so either because they recognized the political advantages (or necessities) therein, or because they viewed participation as a proper thing for a Thaelmann-Pioneers (the children's organization involving nearly all 6- to 14-year-olds in the GDR) to do.[32]

"The Influence of the Youth and Children's Organizations on the Civic Training of School Children" is the subject of a substantial literature in the GDR.[33] A representative example is the work reported by Helmut Stolz and Albrecht Herrmann on the use of group dynamics in school collectives in the achievement of attitudinal change.[34] After rank-ordering students in terms of social prestige, Stolz and Herrmann found that those with high social prestige often did not exhibit positive attitudes toward the societal and educational objectives of their collectives. Since those with high social prestige also tended to have the greatest influence on peer attitudes, it was clear that collectives with undesirable leadership were developing. The transformation of undesirable student leaders into pupils with positive attitudes toward the goals of the collective was the object of Stolz and Herrmann's experimental intervention. Undesirable leaders were taken out of their usual setting and put together with older activists from the Free German Youth (the GDR youth organization corresponding to the Komsomol in the Soviet Union). In one month, the undesirable leaders had been integrated into a positive collective outside the accustomed classroom setting. They emerged from this experience with transformed attitudes—attitudes that were changed in the absence of their usual peer groups. If a goal of school collectives is the train socialist personalities, then it must be asked why and how undesirable leaders appear and maintain their positions among their peers. It would also be interesting to know what happens to the "transformed" leaders after returning to their accustomed settings.

Open questions notwithstanding, it is clear from the work of Wolfgang Kessel,[35] Manfred Vorwerg,[36] and others that controlled use of peer groups is thought to be the most effective way of transmitting the norms of the socialist personality to the youth of the GDR. This is confirmed by experiments such as the one reported by Guenter Kislat, who compared traditional to collective teaching methods.[37] In his preliminary findings, Kislat supported the notion that group norms positively affected the learning process in the sense that it was not the obviously pedagogical means that lead to norm internalization as much as it was the informal, collective techniques of instruction.

A comprehensive overview of the political socialization implications of social psychological and educational research in the GDR cannot be given here. It is clear that changes in attitudes, values, and norms are taking place among school-age youth in the GDR and the general trend is toward the adoption and internalization of norms consistent with those of the socialist personality. However, there remains an apparent gap between the "is" and the "ought" in the pattern of GDR political socialization.

There is nothing in the literature on political socialization in the FRG and GDR that could lead to the conclusion that anything like "democratic" and "socialist" personalities have become dominant in their respective areas. Yet the student and observer cannot ignore the differences that are emerging. Increasingly, one senses that GDR citizens take pride in their society and its accomplishments. A reflection of this attitude "that we are somebody" in the GDR can be found in the important recent analysis of Gebhard Schweigler in his <u>Nationalbewusstsein in der BRD und der DDR</u> (National Consciousness in the FRG and GDR). Following an extensive analysis of the available opinion survey data in East and West, Schweigler sees the rise of a distinct national consciousness in <u>both</u> the FRG and the GDR, while an all-German national identification recedes year by year. Schweigler's data indicate that the youth in the GDR support the state more strongly than do older people, leading to the expectation that support among the population will increase in the future.[38]

Schweigler's findings tend to substantiate the observations of David Childs, Jean Edward Smith, and others who have observed the impact of SED policies since the Berlin Wall.[39] What emerges is a situation burdened with paradoxes. While traditional Prussian symbols and virtues are extolled by the SED leadership in an effort to contrast the disciplined morality of the East with the Americanized decadence of the West, there has been a pronounced trend toward Western consumption patterns. This extends to the Rolex watch on the wrist of the man of affairs, the automobile in the driveway, and if possible, a summer place on a lake. This should not be taken as a sign of convergence with the West; just because elites tend to orient themselves toward the same material symbols does not mean that they are ready to embrace each other.[40]

Recent interviews with GDR youth indicate another paradox in attitudes that show both affirmation and rejection of the socialist personality. In the realm of public attitudes, values consistent with the goals of socialization are revealed· "When one lives in this society and has all its possible advantages, then one must also do something for that society."[41] This accords with the relaxed and open confidence that Western observers noted among the GDR participants at the Tenth World Youth Festival held in Berlin last summer.[42] Yet privately the young people prefer to seek out their own, apart from the state-supervised activities meant to guide leisure time socialization. A nonpolitical area of privacy remains, even among socialized youths in the GDR.

A final paradox is revealed in the attitudes of GDR citizens who may be highly critical of the state, but who nonetheless remain attached and committed to many of the values it represents. This combination of attitudes does not necessarily indicate a longing for the West. Indeed, it can be argued that these people show how profound and lasting the impact of socialization can be. Evidence for this can be found in the literary treatments of the division of Germany such as the novels of Uwe Johnson, which were published in the West after he had left the GDR in 1959. In <u>Zwei Ansichten</u> (Two Views) and

Mutmassungen ueber Jakob (Speculations about Jakob), Johnson tried to show that those in the East think and act differently from those in the West, even though they are not necessarily better people. A complimentary picture emerges from the interviews recorded by Barbara Grunert-Bronnen in Ich bin Buerger der DDR und lebe in der Bundesrepublik (I Am a Citizen of the GDR and Live in the Federal Republic).[43] Repeatedly the interviewees score the anomie of life in the West as contrasted with the supportive collective of the East.

What emerges from these paradoxes and the earlier observations on the socialization process in the FRG and GDR is that the two German states are drawing apart not only politically, but socially and culturally as well. The people in East and West are moving in two incompatible directions. The FRG is moving toward ever closer integration in Western Europe, post-Yom Kippur War developments in the European Community notwithstanding. Socialization processes will continue producing young citizens who are more like their French and British counterparts than their East German "Brothers and Sisters." In the GDR it was recently proclaimed that "the development of all-around, developed socialist personalities is one of the most important tasks of the Party."[44] Clearly the goal of the socialist personality is being pursued with vigor and with increasing impact, while Western influence is fended off by Abgrenzung.

Returning to my opening assumption, it is clear to me that the longer the present trends continue, the more difficult it will be to reunite the two Germanies—should this become a desirable configuration in international affairs. Although it will be a long time before mutually unintelligible languages develop in the FRG and GDR, the diminishing personal ties between people in East and West will strongly reinforce separation. My conclusion here must be that to the extent that political socialization patterns play a role in reunification strategies, that role will be a negative and impeding one in the case of the FRG and the GDR.

NOTES

1. C. L. Sulzberger, "Ostpolitik: Patient Dream," The Oregonian 24 (January 1974): 15.
2. Willy Brandt, "The State of the Nation in Divided Germany," Relay From Bonn (New York: Germany Information Center) 24 January 1974, pp. 5-6.
3. Erich Honecker, Report of the Central Committee to the Eighth Congress of the SED (Dresden: Verlag Zeit im Bild, 1971), p. 17.

4. G. A. Almond and G. B. Powell, Jr., Comparative Politics: A Developmental Approach (Boston: Little, Brown and Co., 1966), p. 24.

5. A. M. Hanhardt, Jr., "Political Socialization in Divided Germany," Journal of International Affairs 27, no. 2 (1973).

6. Karl-Ernst Bungenstab, Umerziehung zur Demokratie? (Duesseldorf: Bertelsmann Universitaetsverlag, 1970).

7. Walter Stahl, ed., Education for Democracy in West Germany (New York: Praeger Publishers, 1961).

8. Ralf Dahrendorf, Society and Democracy in Germany (Garden City: Doubleday, 1967), pp. 75-79.

9. Sidney Verba, "Germany: The Remaking of Political Culture," in Political Culture and Political Development, ed. Lucian W. Pye and Sidney Verba (Princeton, N.J.: Princeton University Press, 1965), p. 165.

10. Elizabeth Noelle and Erich Peter Neumann, eds., The Germans (Allensbach: Verlag fuer Demoskopie, 1967), p. 209.

11. Karl H. Boenner, Deutschlands Jugend und die Erbe ihrer Vaeter (Bergisch Gladbach: Gustav Luebbe Verlag, 1967), p. 222.

12. A. N. Oppenheim, "Attitudes in Civic Education in Several Countries: Development of Cross-National Scales," report submitted by the International Association for the Evaluation of Educational Achievement to UNESCO, May, 1970, p. 16.

13. Judith Gallatin and Joseph Adelson, "Legal Guarantees of Individual Freedom: A Cross-National Study of the Development of Political Thought," Journal of Social Issues 27, no. 2 (1971): 107.

14. Ibid.

15. Hans Weiler, "Schools and the Learning of Dissent Norms: A Study of West German Youths," a paper prepared for delivery at the 1971 Annual Meeting of the APSA, p. 7.

16. See, for example, Gebhard Schweigler, Nationalbewusstsein in der BRD und der DDR (Duesseldorf: Bertelsmann Universitaetsverlag, 1973), pp. 158, 168 and 173.

17. Georg Mende, ed., Ueber die Entwicklung sozialistischer Persoenlichkeiten (Berlin: Deutscher Verlag der Wissenschaften, 1960), pp. 96-97.

18. Protokoll der Verhandlungen des V. Parteitages der SED (Berlin: Dietz Verlag, 1959), pp. 2, 1395.

19. "Gesetz ueber die sozialistische Entwicklung des Schulwesens in der DDR vom 2. Dezember 1959," in Bildungspolitik und Bildungsreform, ed. Leonhard Froese (Munich: Wilhelm Goldmann Verlag, 1969), p. 164.

20. "Gesetz ueber das einheitliche sozialistische Bildungssystem," in Das System der sozialistischen Gesellschafts- und Staatsordnung in der DDR: Dokumente (Berlin: Staatsverlag, 1969), p. 446.

21. Edgar Drefenstedt and Gerhart Neuner, Lehrplanwerk und Unterrichtsgestaltung (Berlin: Volk und Wissen, 1969), pp. 150-51.

22. Walter Friedrich, "Zu Theoretischen Problemen der marxistischen Jugendforschung," Jugendforschung 1/2 (1967), p. 15.

23. Walter Friedrich's principal work is Jugend Heute, 2nd ed. (Berlin: Deutscher Verlag der Wissenschaften, 1967).

24. H. Mueller and H. Schedlich, "Schulklassenspeziefische Bedingungen der politischen Einstellungsbildung," Paedogogik 1 (1966), cited by Adolf Kossakowski, Zur Psychologie der Schuljugend (Berlin: Volk und Wissen, 1969), pp. 150-51.

25. Werner Hennig, "Interessenstrukturen von Jugendlichen," Jugendforschung 5 (1968): 19-33.

26. Kossakowski, op. cit., p. 164.

27. Ulrike Siegel, "Nationale Gruppen im Urteil Jugendlicher," Jugendforschung 3/4 (1967): 103-24.

28. William Buchanan and Hadley Cantril, How Nations See Each Other (Urbana: University of Illinois Press, 1953).

29. Jean Edward Smith, Germany Beyond the Wall (Boston: Little, Brown, and Co., 1969), p. 163.

30. Walter Friedrich and Georg Schmidt, "Experiment zur Urteilsbildung bei Jugendlichen," Jugendforschung 12 (1969): 141.

31. Urie Bronfenbrenner, Two Worlds of Childhood (New York: Russell Sage Foundation, 1970).

32. Arnold Pinther, "Ueber Bedingungen und Massnahmen zur Effektivitaetssteigerung der Jugendweihe," Jugendforschung 9 (1969): 28.

33. G. Neubert et al., "Der Einfluss der Jugend- und Kinderorganisation auf die staatsbuergerliche Erziehung der Schuljugend," in Beitraege zur staatsbuergerlichen Erziehung aelterer Schueler (Berlin: Volk und Wissen, 1968), pp. 198-251.

34. Helmut Stolz and Albrecht Herrmann, Ueber das Kind und seine sozialen Beziehungen in der DDR (Munich: Ernst Reinhardt Verlag, 1966), pp. 71-83.

35. Wolfgang Kessel, Probleme der Lehrer-Schueler-Beziehungen (Berlin: Volk und Wissen, 1969).

36. Manfred Vorwerg, Die Struktur des Kollektivs in sozialpsychologischer Sicht (Berlin: Deutscher Verlag der Wissenschaften, 1970).

37. Guenter Kislat, "Zur Interiorisation verallgemeinter Verhaltensnormen in 9. Klassen (vorlaeufige Mitteilungen)," in Siebenbrodt, ed., Bericht ueber den 2. Kongress der Gesellschaft fuer Psychologie in der DDR (Berlin: Deutscher Verlag der Wissenschaften, 1969), pp. 195-98.

38. Schweigler, op. cit., pp. 99-100 and 195.

39. David Childs, East Germany (New York: Praeger Publishers, 1969); Smith, op. cit.; Peter C. Ludz, "Zum Begriff der 'Nation' in der Sicht der SED," Deutschland Archiv 5, no. 1 (1972): 33-45; and A. M. Hanhardt, Jr., The German Democratic Republic (Baltimore: The Johns Hopkins Press, 1968).

40. Raymond Aron recently warned of the illusion of a convergence which cannot take place until the power monopoly of the state party is broken. This is not likely to happen in the foreseeable future. Interview with Raymond Aron, Der Spiegel 27, no. 36 (3 September 1973): 92.

41. "Privat reden sie ganz anders," Der Spiegel 27, no. 33 (13 August 1973): 36.

42. Die Zeit (Hamburg) 28, no. 32 (10 August 1973): 4-5.

43. Barbara Grunert-Bronnen, Ich bin Buerger der DDR und lebe in der Bundesrepublik (Munich: Piper, 1970)

44. "The development of all-around, developed socialist personalities is one of the most important tasks of the Party . . . ," Neues Deutschland (Berlin) 28, no. 234 (25 August 1973): 10.

CHAPTER 4

INTERNATIONAL INTEGRATION THEORIES AND PROBLEMS OF UNIFYING A DIVIDED NATION: THE CASE OF KOREA

Young Whan Kihl

INTRODUCTION

Throughout the world today there are many nations that are divided: two Germanies, two Koreas, two Vietnams, two Chinas, two Yemens, and so on. Division of the former British colony of India in 1946 into two parts, India and Pakistan (which in turn split into Pakistan and Bangladesh as a result of the war of 1971), may not be atypical of the problems which confront the many newly independent nations of Asia and Africa in making and remaking political unification.[1] The question of what causes nations to be united or divided is difficult to answer because a host of factors are responsible for the phenomenon of political unification. At least one factor can be found in the fact that political division was imposed from outside as a result of the defeat of war, as in Germany, or of war-related circumstances as in Korea following World War II.[2]

The question of unifying divided Korea is not so much the problem of starting anew the process of integrating two heterogenous communities of different origins as that of reuniting or reassociating divided parts of a single national community into one political unit. The task is not necessarily easier, however, because the two Koreas have been under the control of divergent and antagonistic ideological and social systems.[3] During the 27 years of partition of the land, a political regime has emerged in each Korea having vested interests in perpetuating its rule, and the power holders are not likely to relinquish their authority for the sake of achieving political unification. The aspiration for reassociation may be intense and widespread among the elite and mass public alike. Yet, the power elite perception and expectation of reunification of Korea may not be so sacrificial or noble as to relinquish voluntarily their firm political control.[4]

There is hardly anything written about the question of reintegrating or reuniting divided nations, except on a peripheral level.[5] The literature abounds on the question of integrating the communities at the regional level within a nation or between nations.[6] International integration, regional or global, is relevant but not sufficient for the full explanation of reintegrating or reassociating divided nations. Recently it was pointed out that at least four ambiguities underlie the theory of international integration.[7] They are (1) ambiguity of integration as process or condition, (2) the tendency to treat interaction as integration, (3) the failure to distinguish elite from mass integration, and (4) the ambiguity of economic, political, military, and social integration. The process of unifying divided Korea, now under way since 1971, could be appraised from each of these vantage perspectives as well.

My main task is to raise some questions regarding the process and consequences of unifying a divided Korea by examining the current bilateral talks between the North and the South. I shall approach my task by examining the literature of international relations theory to see how and to what extent some of its findings could be applied to the case of reunifying divided Korea. In doing so I will proceed in three steps: first, the relevance of the theory of international integration will be examined in the light of Korean experience; second, the current North-South interaction will be analyzed from the perspective of functional approach to unification; and, third, the alternative strategies of unification, like neofunctionalism and federalism, will be examined.

RELEVANCE AND APPLICABILITY OF INTERNATIONAL INTEGRATION THEORY

Most of the treatises on unification in the discipline of international relations are about the question of how to achieve world unity or regional integration.* The underlying assumptions of the world unity movement and regional integration seem to be based on these propositions. First, given the condition of the world which is divided

---

*The globalist plea of the earlier school, such as the World Federalist movement of the legal bent, has given way gradually to the advocates of regional integration who are more social-science oriented in their focus.

into separate nation-states, the cause of world peace can better be served by bringing "parts and places" together.[8] Second, as the force of science and technology (for example, means of communication and transportation) makes the world much closer and smaller, the needs for political and psychological unity of mankind become even greater.[9] Third, the fact of nationalism and sovereignty in the world today may be a stumbling block in achieving a larger framework for cooperation among the nation-states.[10]

In achieving the objective of world unity and regional integration the students of international relations proceed to specify a number of conditions and factors that are deemed necessary for the integration of existing political units into a larger community. At least three major components or variables of the integration process have been identified: mutual relevance, background conditions, and interaction process.[11] First, there must be a sharing of the sense of mutual relevance and attention-getting exhibited by two or more nations at the level of elite and mass public. Second, there must be present favorable background conditions like geographic proximity, common culture, or similar historical experience, and so on. Third, there must be an increasing degree of interaction, like travel and trade, between governments and population alike in an effort to solve specific problems of mutual concern.* All of these elements seem to apply favorably to the situation of the two Koreas in trying to reunify the divided land.

What makes the case of Korea different from the overall cases in international integration, however, is that here we are dealing with the situation of "re-grouping" or "re-associating" the nation which was arbitrarily divided by external powers.[12] In this sense Korea shares its common characteristics with other divided nations of the world. However, Korea presents itself as a unique situation, even among the many divided nations today, in that there is a high degree of similarity and compatibility of the background conditions which are considered to be essential for integration. The two Koreas already share a series of favorable background conditions like common language, ethnic homogeneity and one culture. The elite and mass aspiration for unification is also very high and intense. The populations of both Koreas also share common expectation, although not necessarily common attitudes on many issues.† The governments in Seoul

---

*World tourism and travel has been recognized as one of the important issues and matters of concern by the UN General Assembly in the recent decision of December 1972.

†Twenty-seven years of separation brought about a state of psychological alienation between the populations of the North and the

and Pyongyang initiated a series of measures, through the Red Cross talks and the North-South Coordinating Committee, to accommodate mutual concern and interest in settling specific problems.

In its outward appearance, therefore, the unification of divided Korea seems to be a foregone conclusion. All the necessary ingredients for a perfect integration are present in the Korean peninsula. Yet, we know that Korean unification is not to be taken for granted as an automatic process or as an easy task; it will come about only as a result of the continuous dialogue and interaction between the two parts of divided Korea. In this respect the case of Korea seems to show that background conditions favorable for integration need to be translated into a series of positive actions and a process of interaction between the two governmental actors. Before moving on to examine relevance of the second and third approaches to the process of unifying divided Korea, perhaps we should elaborate upon specific components of the integration theory to see how and why they do not apply literally to the case of Korea.

There are many outstanding studies on international regional integration.[13] Recently an effort has been made to codify some of the significant findings into a coherent set of propositions.[14] Mainly for the sake of convenience I shall rely on one particular source by Cobb and Elder which is notable for its succinct exposition and summary.[15]

Based on the empirical analysis of 49 nations in the global sample and 15 nations in the North Atlantic sample, Cobb and Elder examined the pattern of interrelationship among the three independent variables of mutual relevance, background conditions, and interaction process. They suggest a number of interesting findings which are of some relevance to the case of unifying divided Korea. They report, for instance, that there are higher correlations among exchanges of communications and goods (trade, mail, telegraph, and so on) than among exchanges of people (tourism, student exchange, and so forth) in the regional study of the North Atlantic area, but this is not necessarily so in the global system.[16] Does this finding mean that the current North-South dialogue should start with the exchange of goods rather than that of people, such as the Red Cross efforts to bring about the unification of dispersed families? Or does the case of two Koreas provide a unique situation whereby the family reunion and exchange of visits take precedence over the exchange of mails and goods?

South in 1971. The only common denominator between the two seems to be the sharing of an aspiration and expectation about the unification of Korea in the distant future.

PROBLEMS OF UNIFICATION: THE CASE OF KOREA

Cobb and Elder also report that geographically more prominent nations tend to show greater mutual relevance in the global system but that proximity and common boundaries are not influential in predicting patterns of mutual relevance in the North Atlantic region.[17] Of course the implication of this finding for the Korean experience is that geography per se does not determine the outcome of unifying divided Korea but that the geographic sharing of common boundary can be utilized and exploited by the leadership for the mutual benefit of both Koreas. Other findings include statements such as: there is a greater mutual relevance and intercourse in the global system (a) if they share the greater common historical attributes, (b) if they are the more homogeneous in terms of culture, socio-economic development and social welfare policies, and (c) if they are the more powerful militarily or economically, and the more similar in terms of bureaucratic capabilities.[18] Each of these propositions can be examined in the context of unifying two Koreas as to their relevance and applicability.

The most interesting finding, which has some bearing on the current North-South dialogue as a means of unifying divided Korea, deals with the question of increasing the level of interaction between two nations. Cobb and Elder report that the more mutually relevant the two nations, the greater their subsequent level of intergovernmental collaboration in both systems.[19] The implication of this finding in the Korean context is that the current negotiation between Seoul and Pyongyang on the intergovernmental level should by all means be encouraged to continue and that the more similar the two Koreas become in all aspects of social experiments, the greater will be the chances of mutual collaboration and interaction. In this respect the recent decision to amend the constitution in South Korea, for purposes of strengthening the executive hand and streamlining the political structure, acquires special meaning and significance.* It appears that both Pyongyang and Seoul have attempted to stabilize the conditions of internal politics and social living in the name of bringing about the task of reunifying the country.

---

*On October 17, 1972 president Park Chung Hee declared martial law in South Korea, ostensibly to bring about a radical change in political structure. The constitutional amendment, subsequently approved by the national referendum, provided for the so-called National Council of Unification and strengthened the position of President Park. Some observers think that the new political structure of South Korea, in terms of the council form of governing, is not dissimilar to the Soviet form of government in North Korea.

FUNCTIONAL APPROACH TO NATIONAL UNIFICATION

The fact that there are two paths towards unification pursued by both Koreas, that is, the Red Cross talks and the North-South Coordinating Committee, is significant in clarifying the question of strategy for integration and unification. The two Koreas are experimenting not only with the so-called functional path of the nonpolitical and humanitarian activities of the Red Cross talks but also with an essentially bilateral political consultation through the North-South Coordinating Committee.[20] The fact that both meetings are held simultaneously and side-by-side may prove to be fruitful in terms of agreeing on important outstanding issues. It appears that there already was a trade-off between the two channels. For instance, the matter of establishing propaganda offices actively debated at the third Red Cross meeting in Pyongyang late in October 1972 was amicably settled following the subsequent visitation to Pyongyang by the South Korean delegation to attend the second meeting of the chairmen of the North-South Coordinating Committee.

The dynamics of interaction between the two Koreas and the strategy of simultaneous negotiation on humanitarian and political issues may prove to be the unique contribution which the Korean case makes toward functional theory of international integration. The literature on functionalism devotes considerable attention to the question of political-nonpolitical separability of human activities.[21] The functionalist argues that it is possible to separate the question of politics and welfare and that to promote the cooperative measures in the nonpolitical functional domain is the correct path and strategy for building the basis of integration and peace.[22] The critics of functionalism argue, on the other hand, that the separability thesis is false and unrealistic.[23] Since the debate tends to proceed on ideological grounds, one cannot hope to settle the question of the separability thesis once and for all. Neofunctionalists come to take the position that it is not only analytically possible but also heuristically convenient to keep the distinction of political and functional, technical domains of international activity.[24] The case of Korea shows that the two domains of the unification process, humanitarian Red Cross talks on specific issues and political consultative meetings, are closely interrelated; yet they tend to be distinct and reinforcing.

There are some indications that a law of dynamic interaction between the two domains, functional and political, is in effect in the case of Korean negotiation. The Red Cross talks on family reunion are kept low-key as functional and humanitarian cooperation and activity of the two governments. Yet it seems unlikely that the Red Cross talks would be called without an initial political decision by

Seoul and Pyongyang and their acquiescence. Likewise, it appears that the agreement on the North-South Joint Communique, especially with regard to the establishment of the coordinating committee, was stimulated by the progress of the Red Cross talks. The July 1972 communique and the North-South Coordinating Committee are political consultations on a higher level that is more sensitive and less open than the Red Cross talks. Strangely, the Red Cross talks tended to attract more popular attention initially and to excite emotions more than the somewhat subdued political and governmental arrangement of the coordinating committee. The picture may change as the latter continues to make headway in the days ahead in terms of opening up discussions on many important and sensitive issue areas.

The experience of the North-South dialogue so far raises a number of interesting questions which are of some theoretical significance and relevance. It seems justifiable to say that the Red Cross talks have elicited the spirit and habit of cooperation between the two negotiating teams of the Red Cross societies in Korea. Quite possibly, the atmosphere and experience of the talks acted to spill over into the political domain of international governmental cooperation culminating in the agreements of the Joint Communique. At the same time the North-South Coordinating Committee seems to act to reinforce and sustain the Red Cross meetings providing policy guidelines and clarifications. In fact this guidance role of the North-South Coordinating Committee was emphasized by both Lee Hu Rak of South Korea and Pak Sung Chul of North Korea, the respective cochairmen, during their press conference following the first and second consultation meetings. In this sense functional and political approaches to integration and unification are closely at work in the case of resolving the Korean unification problem. Therefore, the Korean experience seems to be relevant to the overall development of the functional theory of integration and unification.[25]

NEOFUNCTIONALISM AND ITS APPLICATION

The Korean experience of the North-South dialogue for achieving unification is quite instructive in clarifying some of the problems arising from the process of functional integration. Many students of neofunctionalism find that there are many types and subcategories of the integration process. Nye suggests, for instance, that there are at least four dimensions of integration that need to be kept apart: policy, institutional, attitudinal, and security community.[26] He also makes a distinction among three types of integration: economic, social, and political. It appears that the leadership of Seoul and Pyongyang were successful in maintaining a distinction between (a) the policy and (b) institutional dimensions of the unification process. They also seem to be aware of the necessity of distinguishing the "social" type of problem solving, such as the Red Cross talks on family reunion, and "political" consultation, on the question of unification, such as the activities of the North-South Coordinating Committee.

The North-South Joint Communique of July 4, 1972 was a remarkable document of historical significance in the sense of specifying both principles and the method of achieving Korean Unification.[27] It could be taken as a pledge by the leadership of both Koreas to integrate and coordinate their policies in implementing the task of reunifying divided land. The threefold principle of Korean unification, adopted as the first point, stipulated that unification shall be achieved (1) "through independent Korean efforts without being subject to external imposition of interference," (2) "through peaceful means, and not through the use of force against each other," and (3) by means of "transcending difference in ideas, ideologies, and systems." A remarkable thing is that two regimes, hitherto mutually antagonistic and suspicious, came to accept this principle as the basis of their unification policy toward one another.

Following the Joint Communique a series of further consultations took place between Seoul and Pyongyang to implement one of the key provisions of the agreement, that is, to set up a South-North Coordinating Committee so as "to implement the agreements and solve various problems including unification." Teams of high-level delegates from both Koreas, headed by Lee Hu Pak of South Korea and Pak Sung Chul of North Korea respectively, exchanged visits during October and early December. It was at the third meeting of the chairmen of the Coordinating Committee in Seoul on December 2, 1972 that the North-South Coordinating Committee formally came into being and an agreement was reached to set up a Joint Secretariat to facilitate the function of the committee.*

Perhaps it is premature to make definite observations regarding the significance of the North-South consultation and its achievements so far. Yet, one is tempted to make generalizations based on the experiences so far. The Korean experience so far seems to suggest that there is a beginning of an integration on the policy level, that is, agreement on the fundamental principle of unification, and that the North-South Coordinating Committee could be construed as evidence of "political integration" in progress. If the Joint Secretariat carries out its task energetically, quite possibly we are also witnessing a beginning of the "institutional integration" taking place. Coupled with

---

*Tong-A Ilbo, December 2, 1972.

PROBLEMS OF UNIFICATION: THE CASE OF KOREA 63

the working of the Red Cross joint office in Panmunjom, as agreed upon during the sourth session in Seoul late in November 1972, the machinery of the joint secretariat and the North-South Coordinating Committee may prove to be vital in laying the groundwork for future cooperation and joint efforts in achieving Korean unification.

To recognize that the experiment of the bilateral negotiation so far has been a success, however, should not be construed as minimizing the tremendous difficulties lying ahead. We have yet to see what kind of tasks and authority the North-South Coordinating Committee and its Joint Secretariat will perform and acquire. The progress of the North-South dialogue so far simply means that two governments have agreed to institutionalize the procedures of consultation for undertaking joint projects and for settling specific problems related to the question of unification. The possible areas of joint endeavor include the reduction of the level of tension and military preparedness, the promotion of economic and trade cooperation, the cultural exchange of artists, information and sport teams, the arrangement for the exchange of mail and visitors, and so on.[28] Since there is no guarantee that each side will not try to take advantage of the weakness of the other side, in performing any or all of these tasks, the restoration of confidence and trust must precede the specific acts of contact and interaction. In this regard the caution that interaction does not necessarily lead to integration assumes its relevance and significance.[29] Attitudinal integration must either precede or at least parallel the process of functional cooperation and integration.[30]

Finally, there is the ultimate question of what is the proper form of unification for Korea in the days ahead. All these acts of functional cooperation, in settling specific problems, are simply a means to an end or the process of leading to the destination of Korean unification. Premier Kim Il Sung of North Korea has proposed confederation as an acceptable solution leading to unification of divided Korea. It is not clear what the official line of President Park Chung Hee of South Korea is in this respect.[31] Presumably, the newly founded National Council of Unification will act to legitimize whatever decision and plan the government of President Park comes to adopt. The present indication is that the Seoul government prefers a gradualist and long-term approach to the attainment of Korean unification.

The North Korean perception of unification based on the idea of self-reliance (Juche) and nationalism must be carefully weighed against and balanced with the more earthly and pragmatic approach of South Korean government.[32] The success of Seoul's strategy hinges on at least two factors. First, can Pyongyang be persuaded to take a long-term strategy or can Kim Il Sung afford to wait that long, especially when he is six years older than Park? Second, would the circumstance of East Asian power politics continue to tolerate and favor the move of two Koreas toward unification? Presently, the neighboring countries of Japan, China, the United States and the USSR seem not to be openly against the unification of Korea. However, since Korean unification will bring about a change in the status quo, quite possibly the interest of some country might be adversely affected by it in the days ahead if the balance of power changes. In that case the unification of the Korean peninsula will become increasingly difficult to attain. In short, the timing of reunification efforts will be crucial.

NOTES

1. The process of new nations emerging out of the former European domination is succinctly described in Rupert Emerson, From Empire to Nation (Cambridge, Mass.: Harvard University Press, 1960).

2. On the origin of the division of Korea following World War II, see Soon Sung Cho, Korea in World Politics: 1940-1950 (Berkeley, Calif.: University of California Press, 1967).

3. The contrast of two systems of North and South Korea is well depicted in Bae-ho Han, "Toward a Comparative Analysis of the South and North Korean Political Systems," Asiatic Studies Journal 15 (March 1972).

4. A study of party elite perception of the unification problem in 1972 is examined briefly in Y. Kihl, "Leadership and Opposition Role Perception of Party Elite," Mimeographed (Prepared for delivery at the 1973 Annual Meeting of the Association for Asian Studies).

5. For instance, on German reunification, see Hans J. Morgenthau, "The Problem of German Reunification," The Annals of the American Academy of Political and Social Sciences 330 (July 1960). Etzioni's work does not deal with the question of reuniting divided nations as such. Amitai Etzioni, Political Unification (New York: Holt, Rinehart and Winston, 1965).

6. For instance, see: J. Jacob and J. Toscano, eds., The Integration of Political Communities (Philadelphia: Lippincott, 1964); Karl Deutsch et al., Political Community and the North Atlantic Area (Princeton, N.J.: Princeton University Press, 1957); Ernst Haas, The Uniting of Europe (Palo Alto, Cal.: Stanford University Press, 1958).

7. Edwin Fedder and Frederic Pearson, "Four Ambiguities of International Integration," in Political Science Annual. Volume Three—1972, ed. James A. Robinson (New York: The Bobbs-Merrill Co., 1972), pp. 281-338.

8. For instance, see J. S. Nye, Peace in Parts: Integration and Conflict in Regional Organization (Boston: Little, Brown and Co., 1971).

9. For instance, see Reinhold Niebuhr, The Children of Light and the Children of Darkness (New York: Charles Scribner's Sons, 1944); and especially the chapter on "The World Community." Also, Reinhold Niebuhr, The Structure of Nations and Empires (New York: Charles Scribner's Sons, 1959).

10. David Mitrany, A Working Peace System (New York: Oxford University Press, 1943, 1966).

11. Karl Deutsch, Political Community at the International Level: Problems of Definition and Measurement (Garden City: Doubleday, 1954); also, Karl Deutsch, Nationalism and Social Communication (Cambridge, Mass.: MIT Press, 1966).

12. The process of "reassociation," rather than unification, as the proper focus of approaching Korean unification was emphasized by Professor Z. Brzezinski in 1970; see Proceedings of the International Conference on the Problems of Korean Unification (Seoul, 1971).

13. In addition to the sources already cited, see L. Lindberg, The Political Dynamics of European Economic Integration (Palo Alto, Calif.: Stanford University Press, 1963); J. Nye, "East African Economic Integration," International Political Communities (Garden City, New York· Anchor, 1966).

14. For instance, Fedder and Pearson, op. cit.

15. Roger W. Cobb and Charles Elder, International Community: A Regional and Global Study (New York: Holt, Rinehart and Winston, 1970).

16. Ibid., pp. 134-35.

17. Ibid.

18. Ibid.

19. Ibid.

20. For the exposition of functional approach to international integration, see: Mitrany, op. cit., and James P. Sewall, Functionalism and World Politics (Princeton, N.J.: Princeton University Press, 1966).

21. For instance, see Inis L. Claude, Swords Into Plowshares: The Problems and Progress of International Organization (New York: Random House, 1964), pp. 318-43.

22. The chief spokesman of this position is Mitrany, op. cit.

23. For instance, see Claude, op. cit.

24. Ernst B. Haas, Beyond the Nation-State (Palo Alto, Calif.: Stanford University Press, 1964).

25. The theme of theoretical implication of Korean experience will further be elaborated in a forthcoming book: Korea and the Politics of Reunification.

26. Nye, Peace in Parts, op. cit., p. 49.

27. Elsewhere, I have examined the July 4, 1972 Joint Communique in detail; see Y. Kihl, "North-South (Korea) Relations: Unification?" Mimeographed. (Prepared for delivery at the Fourth Conference on Korea, Kalamazoo, Michigan, November 10-11, 1972), pp. 9-11.

28. For specific suggestions of functional cooperation between the South and the North, see: Y. Kihl, "Functional Approach to North-South Reassociation," Buk Han (North Korea) 1, no. 10 (October 1972): 88-99.

29. Fedder and Pearson, op. cit.

30. Nye, Peace in Parts, p. 49.

31. Definitely, the Seoul government is opposed to the scheme of neutralization of Korea. For a succinct analysis of why the North Korean proposal for federation is not acceptable to South Korea, see Pyong-Choon Hahn, "Federalism: A Means for the National Reunification of Korea," Proceedings of the International Conference, op. cit., pp. 937-49.

32. I have given further analysis of the North-South negotiating behavior elsewhere. Y. Kihl, "North-South Relations," op. cit., pp. 15-18; also, Y. Kihl, "Korean Response to Major Power Reapproachment," in Young C. Kim (ed.), Major Powers and Korea (Silver Spring: Research Institute on Korean Affairs, 1973).

CHAPTER 5

UNIFICATION OR CONFRONTATION: AN ASSESSMENT OF FUTURE RELATIONS BETWEEN MAINLAND CHINA AND TAIWAN

Yung Wei

One of the most significant developments in world politics since the end of World War II has been the emergence of a huge communist political system on the Chinese mainland as well as the continuing existence of a viable Chinese Nationalist polity on the island of Taiwan. The competition and confrontation between these two mutually hostile systems created a host of thorny problems for other members of the international community until 1971, such as China's representation in the United Nations, the question of diplomatic relations and recognition, and not infrequently, the probability of a renewed civil war which might involve major powers of the world.

The admission of the People's Republic of China (PRC) into the United Nations in October 1971, did not bring about a solution of the problem. For although the Republic of China (ROC) was excluded from the United Nations, and is receiving recognition from a diminishing number of nations, the ROC on Taiwan shows no sign of giving up its long struggle against the Chinese Communists. With a booming economy, a strong armed force ranked the sixth or seventh in the world, and an international trade exceeding that of mainland China, the ROC is still a political force that must be reckoned with in the balance of political, economic, and military powers in East Asia.[1]

Will the ROC and PRC make some efforts toward a peaceful resolution of their conflicts in the near future? Will the PRC make military attempts to attack Taiwan? Conversely, how much probability is there that the ROC will launch a counterattack against mainland China? Aside from military conquest from either side of the Taiwan Strait, is there any possibility of peaceful unification or integration of the two political systems at some point in the future? Furthermore, which factors are contributing to such a unification or integration and

68   THE POLITICS OF DIVISION, PARTITION, AND UNIFICATION

which are against it? These are some of the questions that are frequently raised by scholars, journalists, businessmen, and governmental officials concerned with future development in that part of the world.

Obviously, given the complexities of the relationship between the ROC and the PRC, and the fluid state of international politics at the present time, no scholar who is concerned about the credibility of his predictions would jump to quick conclusions about any of the above-mentioned questions. The purpose of this paper, therefore, is not to give direct, simple answers to any of these questions, but (1) to review the historical developments between the PRC and the ROC (2) to compare the situation between the two Chinese regimes with those of other divided nations (3) to examine the factors for unification and separation and (4) finally, to present some assessments for the future.

THE RELATIONSHIP BETWEEN THE ROC AND THE PRC: A BRIEF HISTORICAL REVIEW

The division of China into two hostile parts in 1949 resulted from a prolonged struggle between the Chinese Nationalists and Chinese Communists. The establishment of a People's Republic of China by the Communists on mainland China in October 1950, coupled with the existence and functioning of the government of the ROC on Taiwan, created a situation wherein each of the two political systems claimed to be the sole legitimate government of the whole China.

In order to appreciate the nature of the relationship between the PRC and the ROC, a brief review of the history of post-1949 China is needed. The relationship between the PRC and the ROC since 1950 can be roughly divided into three periods.[2] The years 1950 to 1953 represented a period of continued military confrontation between the Nationalists and Communists, yet with an increasing tendency toward a stalemate between the two competing groups. When the Nationalists withdrew from mainland China to Taiwan in December 1949, few Western political observers believed that the ROC could exist as an independent political entity for an extended period of time. The political situation in Taiwan as well as the international environment, and especially the unconcerned attitude of the United States toward Taiwan at the time, seemed to support their observations.

The opening of the Korean War in June, 1953, changed the whole picture. The war brought about a quick shift in U.S. policy toward Taiwan—from one of "let the dust settle" to one of active concern. The Seventh Fleet was ordered by President Truman to patrol the

UNIFICATION OR CONFRONTATION: PRC AND TAIWAN

Taiwan Strait to prevent a Communist invasion of the island. It also served to prevent a similar attempt by the Nationalists to attack mainland China.

Despite the patrolling of the Taiwan Strait by the U.S. Seventh Fleet, military confrontations between the PRC and the ROC continued. Among the more serious conflicts between the two were: the attack of Tung-shan Island (of Kwangtung Province of mainland China) by the Nationalists in 1953; the attack, and eventually the occupation, of the Nationalist-held Ta-chen Islands (of Che Kiang Province) by the Communists in 1955, and the severe bombardment of Quemoy and Katsu by the Communists in 1953. Except for communist shelling of the Island of Quemoy in 1953, which almost led to a large scale military confrontation between the ROC and the PRC, with even the possible involvement of the United States, most of the military conflicts between the Nationalists and Communists were of moderate scale and fought in limited areas along the coastal regions of the southwestern part of mainland China.

With the subsidence of the Quemoy Crisis, the relationship between the PRC and the ROC entered into a new stage in 1959. From this year onward, except for a ritualistic exchange of artillery fire on odd-numbered days between the Nationalists on Quemoy and the Communists on the mainland, there has been little military conflict between the two hostile political systems.[3] Therefore, it may be said that a de facto cease-fire has been in existence in the Taiwan Strait since 1959.

It should be pointed out, however, that in the middle of 1962, the government of the ROC did seem to be making a serious effort to prepare for a counterattack against the PRC on mainland China. In May of that year, the Nationalist government announced a special defense budget totalling 60 million U.S. dollars to run through June, 1963. A number of newspaper editors in Taipei speculated that the budget was to cover military expenses for a counterattack against the Communists. The plan was cancelled by the Nationalists, reportedly because of lack of support from the United States.

Although the low level of military confrontation between the Nationalists and Communists has persisted up to the time of this writing, the rapprochement between the United States and the PRC since 1971 has turned the tide of a recently intensified diplomatic warfare in favor of the Chinese Communists. In addition to seating its delegation in the United Nations, the PRC has succeeded in increasing its diplomatic ties with other nations from less than 60 in late 1971 to more than 80 at present. On the other hand, the number of nations recognizing the ROC has dwindled from more than 60 to about 40 during the same period. The Chinese Communists apparently are trying to isolate the Chinese Nationalists to the point where the latter will eventually become a nonpolitical entity in international relations. In addition to its diplomatic offensive, economic as well as all-out psychological warfare is also being waged against the Chinese Nationalists by the Communists. Hence it may be observed that in the near future the struggle between the Communists and the Nationalists will most likely not be characterized by military confrontation but rather by diplomatic, economic, and psychological warfare.

THE PRC VERSUS THE ROC: COMPARISON WITH OTHER DIVIDED NATIONS

Relations between the divided nations of the world share certain common features such as ideological cleavage along a communist-anticommunist line, military alliance with opposing super powers of the world, frequent border incidents coupled with occasional large-scale military confrontations, and continuous espionage and sabotage activities against each other. The situation between the ROC and the PRC, nevertheless, does have several distinct features. First, the division of China into two opposing parts was not the outcome of any international settlement, but was, as previously pointed out, the result of a civil war. Despite the effort made by many nations, including the United States, to ascertain that the status of Taiwan be settled under international law,[5] both the ROC and the PRC have vehemently claimed that there is one China and that Taiwan belongs to China.[6] For both the Nationalists and the Communists, the problem is not whether there is one China, but rather, which government is the legitimate representative of all the people of China.

After many years of resistance the U.S. government finally yielded to the idea of one China including Taiwan. In the Nixon-Chou communique issued in Shanghai on February 29, 1972,[7] it was stated that

> The U.S. side declared: The United States acknowledged that Chinese on either side of the Taiwan Straits maintain there is but one China and that Taiwan is part of China. The United States does not challenge that position. It reaffirms its interest in a peaceful settlement of the Taiwan question by the Chinese themselves. With this prospect in mind, it affirms the ultimate objective of the withdrawal of all U.S. forces and military installations from Taiwan. In the meantime, it will progressively reduce its forces and military installations on Taiwan as the tension in the area diminishes.

TABLE 6

The Divided Nations: Comparative Data on Territory, Population, GNP, and Per Capita Income

	Territory under Control		Population in 1970 (in millions)		GNP (1970) (in billions of U.S. dollars)	Per Capita Income (1970) (in billions of U.S. dollars)
	Thousands Sq. Mi.	Percent of Total	Figure	Percent of Total		
China						
PRC (mainland)	3,700	99.62	800.0	98.2	120.0	145
ROC (Taiwan)	14	0.38	14.6	1.8	6.2	410
Germany						
FRG (West)	96	59.6	61.7	78.3	146.0	2,874
GDR (East)	42	30.4	17.1	21.7	—	—
Korea						
North	47	55.3	14.5	31.3	2.9	230
South	38	44.7	31.8	68.7	7.8	245
Vietnam						
North	61	47.7	20.0	52.6	1.6	90
South	67	52.3	18.0	47.4	3.1	175

Source: World Data Handbook, General Foreign Policy Series 264 (Washington, D.C.: U.S. Department of State, 1972).

By making the above statement, the United States seemed to have abandoned the idea of two Chinas, or of one China, one Taiwan. But it does leave room for the United States to support in one China two mutually hostile political systems.[8] It also does not rule out the possibility that the United States may change its position if, at some time in the future, Chinese on either side of the Taiwan Strait decide that there could be two equally legitimate Chinese nations.

A second unique feature of the PRC/ROC relationship is found in the extremely disproportionate division of territory and population between the two systems. As figures in Table 10.1 demonstrate, of all other divided nations there is approximately equal division of territory and population. Even in the case of the two Germanies, the East Germans still possess 30.4 percent of the territory and 21.7 percent of the population. Yet, in the case of ROC versus PRC the ROC shares only 0.38 percent of the total size of what is considered the territory of China, and merely 1.8 percent of the population. Simply by looking at these figures, the imbalance of territorial base and population size between the Nationalists and Communists seems to assume an enormous proportion. It must be pointed out, nevertheless, that the Chinese Nationalists have made extremely good use of the limited geographical base at their disposal and have developed it into a sizable industrial complex. As a result, the ROC has been able to achieve a volume of trade of over 5 billion U.S. dollars in 1972, which was more than the estimated foreign trade of the Communist Chinese. With this economic base and with a population of more than 15 million, which is larger than the population of more than 60 percent of the nations of the world, the ROC has been able to maintain a modern armed force 600,000 men strong.

Other than the prolonged civil war and the discrepancies on territory and population size, a third important difference in the relationships between the ROC and the PRC and those between other divided nations is that there is the some one-hundred-mile-wide Taiwan Strait between the ROC and the PRC. This is not the case between any of the other divided nations. The existence of such a natural barrier poses a serious challenge to any Communist attempt to take Taiwan. It also, at the same time, creates problems for the Nationalists in terms of logistic support should they attempt to counterattack mainland China.

Finally, the nearly 20 million Chinese overseas constitute another unique problem in the relationship between the Nationalists and the Communists. These 20 million Chinese overseas spread all over the world, although the overwhelming majority of them are found in Southeast Asia. Despite the efforts made by the governments of their residing societies, many of the overseas Chinese are still identified with the governments in China; the problem is, which China?

Here one finds the most fervent competition between the ROC and the PRC for loyalty among the Chinese overseas. Until most recently, the ROC seemed to be able to command support from the majority of the overseas Chinese who still look to China for their political identity. Recent developments in the international arena, however, seem to have given the Chinese Communists an opportunity to erode the overseas Chinese support for the Nationalists. In any case, the allegiance of the Chinese overseas will continue to play an important role in the competition and conflict between the ROC and the PRC.

UNIFICATION OR CONTINUING SEPARATION: AN ANALYSIS OF ALTERNATIVES

Having presented a brief review of the history of confrontation between the ROC and the PRC as well as identifying some of the unique features of PRC-ROC relations, some assessment of the possible developments between two political systems is in order. Theoretically speaking, there could be at least four possible developments in the relations between mainland China and Taiwan, including (1) a peaceful unification of mainland China and Taiwan into a single political entity, (2) military unification either through the conquest of Taiwan by the Communists, or through the repossession of mainland China by the Nationalists in a counterattack, (3) the emergence of a Taiwanese nation, separate from mainland China, and (4) the continuation of the status quo.

Let us first examine the possibility of a peaceful unification. Karl Deutsch, Ernst Haas, and Lucian Pye have all investigated the conditions for uniting different political units into a single political entity.[9] Among the conditions that have been considered by these scholars as conducive to a peaceful political integration and unification are the sharing of a common memory and basic socio-cultural values, socio-economic interdependence, an accommodating attitude toward unification among the political elites of the various units, and mutual responsiveness based upon past experience. Judging by these criteria, the possibilities of a peaceful unification of the PRC and the ROC into a single political entity in the foreseeable future is very slim.

In terms of the sharing of a common memory, recent survey research has shown that despite the more than 20 years of separation, the people of mainland China and Taiwan still share a rather similar socio-political culture.[10] There are certain differences in the interaction patterns between the mainlanders and Taiwanese, but these differences did not create serious cleavages in their cultural and political outlook.[11] Merely looking at these data, one may

TABLE 7

Mainland China Versus Taiwan: A Comparison
of Standard of Living (1969-70)

	Mainland China	Taiwan
Adult literacy	About 40 percent	83 percent
Labor force	350,000,000	4,300,000
Agricultural	85 percent	43 percent
Industrial and other	15 percent	57 percent
Gross national product	$80 billion	$6 billion
GNP per capita	$100	$329
Crude steel per capita	33 lbs	64.4 lbs
Telephones per capita	1:3,380	1:53
Radios per capita	1:145	1:10
Food: per capita daily		
Calorie intake	1,780	2,670
Protein intake	30	70

Sources: Issues in United States Foreign Policy: Nov. 4, Communist China (Washington, D.C.: Dept. of State, 1969), p. 14; 1968 Taiwan Demographic Fact Book (Taichung, Taiwan: Dept. of Civil Affairs, Taiwan Provincial Government, 1969); Facts About Free China (Taipei, Taiwan: China Publishing Company, 1969); China Year Book, 1969-1970 (Taipei, Taiwan: China Publishing Company, 1970); and data reported by Central Daily News, Dec. 27, 1971, p. 1.

come to the conclusion that there would be little problem in uniting the people of mainland China and those of Taiwan. But possessing similar cultural-political traits is one thing, accepting different political ideology and the rule of a different political authority is quite another. Judging from the continuous flow of refugees from mainland China to the outside world, it is not feasible to expect that the people of Taiwan would be willing to accept the communist ideology and join a political system from which many people are so eager to get out.

One of the basic factors that discourages the unification of Taiwan with the mainland is the much higher standard of living enjoyed by the Chinese people on Taiwan than that of their compatriots in mainland China. As data in Table 7 reveal, the standard of living of the people of Taiwan is far higher than that of mainland China. This is testified to by a higher adult literacy rate, more industrial and commercial population, higher per capita income, higher calorie per capita intake, and higher incidence of the possession of radios and telephones. Despite a recent claim made by Chou En-lai to the contrary,[12] most likely the people of modernized Chinese society on Taiwan[13] will probably have a lower standard of living if the island is incorporated in the state-controlled economy of Communist China.

In terms of the attitude of the ruling elites, there exist great mutual distrust and hostility between the Chinese Nationalists and Communists. This is an outgrowth of more than 40 years of life-and-death struggle between two opposing political elites. There has been no lack of experience of negotiations and even collaboration between the Nationalists and the Communists. Yet each of these experiences ended with bitter mutual accusation followed by more intensified conflicts.[14] Since late 1971 the Chinese Communists have launched a peace offensive against the Nationalists. It took the form of inviting scholars of Chinese origin to visit mainland China, inducing procommunist nationalism among the overseas Chinese students over the Tia-Ya Tai Incident,[15] making proposals for peaceful resolution of the Taiwan question through a third, usually procommunist, party, and intensified broadcasts to the Nationalist-held offshore islands. Thus far, all the so-called "peace" overtures of the Chinese Communists have been met with stiff opposition and rejection by the Nationalists. The government of the ROC has recently reaffirmed its intention to stay in the democratic camp and to continue the national goal of the recovery of mainland China.[16]

If a peaceful unification of mainland China and Taiwan is not currently feasible, how about unification through a military confrontation between the Nationalists and Chinese Communists? The probability of this happening is also very small. On the part of the Nationalists, they fully realize the military imbalance between themselves and the Communists, although they also believe that they have a better trained and equipped armed force. For this reason, the Nationalists have thus far refrained from any all-out military action against the Communists, but stress the principle of "seventy percent political struggle, and thirty percent military confrontation," to fulfill their goal of national unification.[17] A Nationalist counterattack will be more likely if a large-scale military conflict occurs between the PRC and the USSR, or a serious and violent struggle over succession happens among various contenders after Mao's death, or the local military commanders in Fukien and Kwangtung Provinces in Southern China rebel against the central authority in Peking and seek assistance from the Nationalists in Taiwan.

As for the Communists, their much larger military force of 2.8 million is scattered throughout the vast territories of mainland China.[18] Prevention of a Russian attack in the Sinkiang province and Manchuria absorbed almost half of the military might of the Chinese

Communists. Consequently, the amount of force which the Chinese Communists could use for a military adventure in Taiwan is seriously limited. The likelihood of a communist attack against Taiwan will increase if the conflicts between the PRC and the USSR are significantly reduced, or if the United States severs diplomatic ties with Taiwan and renounces the mutual defense treaty protecting the island, or if internal conflict or civic disturbance occur in Taiwan. At the present, none of the above conditions is likely to develop. Some of the China experts are even of the opinion that the Chinese Nationalists are able to defend themselves militarily without active U.S. participation.[19] From the above analyses, we may conclude that the probability of a forced unification of mainland China and Taiwan through military action is quite small.

If neither peaceful unification nor military confrontation is feasible in the near future, how about the establishment of a Taiwanese nation on the island as a "permanent" solution to the problem? The answer to this question is that after UN admission and the recognition of Peking by many nations as the government of all China, it does not make much difference whether the people on the island of Taiwan officially declare their independence or not. It is not likely that the ROC can regain their seat in the UN General Assembly after such a declaration of independence, nor will it win diplomatic recognition with countries which have already recognized mainland China. For the communist part, they may better tolerate a hostile but nevertheless Chinese political system on Taiwan than a legally independent Taiwanese nation separate from China.

For many years there has been a separatist movement supported by certain Taiwanese intellectuals who are dissatisfied with the Nationalist rule on Taiwan.[20] Since the organizations and the activities of the so-called "Formosan (Taiwanese) Independence Movement" (FIM) are rather secretive, it is hard to assess the strength and the membership of the organization. It is known, however, that the major operational bases of the movement are found in Japan and in the United States.

Since the Nixon-Chou Shanghai Communique and since the recognition of the PRC by Japan, the FIM has been faced with serious problems of ideological confusion and internal factional divisions. The Chinese Communists have made some efforts to recruit the left wing of the FIM, yet without much success. With diminishing hope for support from either the United States or Japan, and with an increasing communist threat against Taiwan, it is very likely that many of the members of FIM will seek reconciliation with the Chinese Nationalists to keep Taiwan a noncommunist society.[21]

From the foregoing analysis, it is clear that the most likely course of development in the relations between mainland China and

Taiwan is the continuation of a stalemate in the struggle for hegemony between the PRC and the ROC. Most likely, the struggle will take the form of intensified diplomatic, economic, and psychological warfare between the two political systems. As of this moment, the primary concern of the Chinese Communists seems to be the threat from the Soviet Union. As for the Chinese Nationalists, they are naturally more preoccupied with the threat coming from across the Taiwan Strait. Yet, with a booming economy, a combat-ready armed force, and an enlarged political base through a series of national, provincial, and local elections, held recently on the island, the government and the people of the ROC seem to be more determined than ever before to defend the fruits of their modernization efforts on Taiwan. They further hope that, through their determined efforts, their compatriots in mainland China may also share these fruits of success with them someday.[22]

NOTES

1. See Yung Wei, "Political Development in the Republic of China on Taiwan," in China and the Question of Taiwan: Documents and Analysis, ed. Hungdah Chiu (New York: Praeger, 1973), pp. 74-111.
2. For a more detailed discussion on the various stages of confrontation between the ROC and the PRC, especially in relation to the developments in the ROC, see Wei, op. cit., pp. 76-83.
3. "Future of Taiwan," Editorial Research Reports (May 26, 1972), p. 410.
4. See Wei, op. cit., p. 84.
5. Arthur H. Dean, "United States Foreign Policy and Formosa," Foreign Affairs 33 (April, 1955); J. P. Jain, "The Legal Status of Formosa, A Study of British, Chinese and Indian Views," American Journal of International Law 57 (1963); and Quincy Wright, "The Chinese Recognition Problem," American Journal of International Law 49 (1963).
6. For a rebuttal of the opinions of the "undetermined" status of Taiwan, see Hung-dah Chiu, "The Legal Status of Taiwan and Penghu," in H. D. Chiu, Selected Problems of Modern International Law (Taipei: New Century Publishing Co., 1966), pp. 97-111.
7. As reprinted in Chiu, op. cit., p. 346.
8. For a more elaborate discussion on this, see Yung Wei, "Political Development in the Republic of China on Taiwan: Analysis and Projections," paper delivered at the International Symposium on the future of Taiwan, Arizona State University, Tempe, Arizona, February 2-3, 1973.

9. For a sample of the ideas of these scholars, see Karl W. Deutsch, Political Community at the International Level (Garden City, N.Y.: Doubleday and Co., 1954); K. W. Deutsch, Nationalism and Social Communication. An Inquiry into the Foundation of Nationality (Cambridge, Mass.: M.I.T. Press, 1955); Ernst B. Haas, The Uniting of Europe (Stanford, Calif.: Stanford University Press, 1958); Lucian W. Pye, Politics, Personality, and Nation-Building (New Haven, Conn.: Yale University Press, 1962).

10. These are unveiled by recent studies on the Chinese political culture and political socialization process on Taiwan; see, for example, Richard H. Solomon, Mao's Revolution and the Chinese Political Culture (Berkeley, Calif.: University of California Press, 1971); Sheldon Appleton, "Taiwanese and Mainlanders on Taiwan," op. cit.; Richard W. Wilson, "A Comparison of Political Attitudes of Taiwanese Children and Mainlander Children on Taiwan," Asian Survey 8 (Dec. 1968): 980-1000; and Richard W. Wilson, "The Learning of Political Symbols in Chinese Culture," Journal of Asian and African Studies 3 (July-October 1968): 246-54.

11. Appleton, op. cit.; and Wilson, op. cit.

12. In a recent interview with a group of overseas Chinese scholars visiting mainland China, Chou claimed that after unification with mainland China, the living standard of the people of Taiwan would not drop, but would be further raised. See Kan Ts'ai, "A Report on the Meeting Between Chou En-lai and A Group of Taiwanese," Ch'i-shih Nien-Tai (1970s), Hong Kong 35 (Dec. 1972): 38-39.

13. For the rapid pace of modernization on Taiwan, see Yung Wei, "Taiwan: A Modernizing Chinese Society," in Taiwan in Modern Times, ed. Paul K. T. Sih (Jamaica, N.Y.: St. John's University Press, 1973).

14. For the Nationalist version of the unsatisfactory experience of collaborating with the Chinese Communists, see Chiang Kai-Shek, Soviet Russia In China (New York: Farrar, Straus and Co., 1957); for an account of an American experience, see Kenneth T. Young, Negotiating with the Chinese Communists (New York: McGraw-Hill Book Company, 1968).

15. The Chinese Communists seemed to have used the pro-communist student publications in the United States as one of the major instruments for peace offensives. See, for example, "It is Time for the Nationalists and the Communists to Negotiate," Yeh Ts'so (Wild Weeds) 12 (November 15, 1972): 1-3; also some magazines in Hong Kong were used as sounding boards. For example, see Kan Ts'si, op. cit.

16. In a report made to the Legislative Yuan on September 29, 1972, Premier Chiang Ching-Kuo stated that the overall goals of anti-communism and national recovery of the ROC will never be changed.

See "ROC Policies Won't Change," Free China Weekly (Taipei) (October 1, 1972): 1. Chiang again stated on January 22, 1973 that the government of the ROC will never negotiate with the Chinese Communists; see Chung-Yang Jih-Pao (Central Daily News), Taipei (January 23, 1973), p. 1.

17. See Chiang Ching-Kuo's explanation reported in Chung-Yang Jih-Pao (January 23, 1973), p. 1.

18. For the allocation of military forces in mainland China, see The Military Balance 1969-1970 (London: The Institute for Strategic Studies, 1969), pp. 39-40; also see, "The Military Balance, 1972/73," Air Force (December, 1972): 86. Also cf. James H. Buck, "Military Power—China and Japan," paper delivered at Forty-Fourth Annual Meeting of Southern Political Science Association, Atlanta, Georgia, Nov. 2-4, 1972.

19. For example, see Jerome Alan Cohen, "Recognizing China," Foreign Affairs (October, 1971): 38.

20. For a discussion on the background and the goals of the Formosan Independence Movement, see Douglas Mendel, The Politics of Formosan Nationalism (Berkeley, Calif.: University of California Press, 1970).

21. See Douglas Mendel, "Formosan Nationalist Movement in Crisis," paper delivered at the International Symposium on the Future of Taiwan, Arizona State University, Tempe, Arizona, February 2-3, 1973.

22. Robert A. Scalapino once suggested that it would be an advantage to have a Chinese government successful in its economic and social politics at home and also keeping traditional Chinese civilization alive along with prosperity and freedom. See Scalapino, "The Question of Two Chinas," in China in Crisis, Vol. 2, ed. Tang Tacu (Chicago: University of Chicago Press, 1968), p. 126.

CHAPTER 6

BANGLADESH: THE PRICE OF NATIONAL UNITY
Kathleen Knight

ALTERNATIVES TO NATIONALISM?

Bangladesh was first recognized as an independent nation-state on December 4, 1971—a little more than nine months after the first reports of atrocities against the people of East Bengal began to reach the press of the United States and Western Europe, and almost exactly a year after the Awami League led by Majibar Rahman finalized an electoral victory which would have insured East Pakistani dominance in the new National Assembly of Pakistan. The spectacular emergence of Bangladesh into the nation-state system has prompted numerous questions, of which perhaps the most important concerns the inability of the elaborate machinery of the United Nations, including its Commission on Human Rights and Sub-Commission on Prevention of Discrimination and Protection of Minorities, to act in the face of mounting evidence of gross violations of human rights in East Pakistan (Salzberg, 1973).

Stanley Hoffman suggested several years ago that ". . . the fragmentation of the world into countless units, each of which has a claim to independence, is obviously dangerous for peace and illogical for welfare." (1968: 177) The failure of the United Nations in the case of Bangladesh is intimately connected to the concept of national sovereignty. That the creation of a nation-state is the only response which the international community offers for a situation such as Bangladesh is pathetic. It does little for the people of Bangladesh, and even less for the people of the world in general, reinforcing, as it does, the notion that:

nation-states—often inchoate, economically absurd, administratively ramshackle, and impotent yet dangerous in international politics—remain the basic units . . . not only do they profit from man's incapacity to bring about a better order, but their very existence is a formidable obstacle to their replacement. (Hoffman, 1968: 178)

In his book <u>Nationalism and Its Alternatives</u> (1969), Karl Deutsch proposed that the two main variables influencing assimilation are language, or more broadly "interlocking habits of communication" (p. 14) and the expectation that demands would be met, or the "probability of mutual trust." (p. 16) He foresaw that a kind of demand overload would occur when social mobilization developed at a greater rate than assimilation (p. 29), and suggested that only an innovative elite capable of meeting multiple new demands would be able to maintain the viability of the nation-state. (p. 89) It is questionable, however, whether such an elite could maintain a state under such circumstances, and, moreover, is it realistic to expect such a competent and effective elite to be present or develop? The independence of Bangladesh can be seen as a demonstration of the nonviability of the 1947-71 Pakistani nation-state. Choudhury (1975) places the blame directly upon certain of the elite, including both Rahman and Bhutto, as well as the prominent Pakistani generals. Ali (1970), who maintains that the Bengali struggle was essentially against colonial domination by the West Wing, agrees with this interpretation. He further suggests that it was the political ineptitude and corruption of the West Pakistani ruling class after the death of Jinnah and the assassination of Liaquat Ali Khan that led to the military takeover under Ayub Kahn.

Jahan (1972), taking a more detached and scholarly approach, still concludes that the policies of the Ayub regime (1958-68) were responsible for the alienation of East Bengal. She suggests: "The prime necessity of the state's survival as an independent international entity often pushes the governing elite to concentrate on state-building at the cost of nation-building." (1972: 3) This results in an overemphasis on the establishment of a strong central authority, an efficient administrative system, economic development and "law and order" at the expense of nascent political processes which must be encouraged in order to promote assimilation in the Deutschian sense.

There is agreement that the ruling elite of Pakistan was incapable of providing the kind of innovative leadership necessary to maintain a united Pakistan. However, there is disagreement over whether any elite could be capable of holding together a nation-state with the unique problems of Pakistan. Ali, whose book was published prior to the crisis, maintained that Bengali independence was inevitable. Jahan recognizes that emphasis on state-building was in many respects dictated by the characteristics of the international system to which Pakistan belonged, even though this emphasis was bound to be destructive of the very union it sought to preserve.

Pakistan—the Pakistan of 1947-71—was a curious example of a divided nation because it was divided not only by language and race but by geography as well. An important part of the national ideology of Pakistan rested on the principle that a nation so divided could be held together by a common religion—or more basically by a common fear of another, more numerous, religious group. The reluctance on the part of some Pakistanis to accept the inevitability of Bengali independence may reflect a deeper fear that if the principle did not hold between the East and West it would not hold within it.

A BRIEF PRE-HISTORY

The Indian subcontinent has suffered only three invasions of consequence in a recorded history beginning in about 3000 B.C.: a Hellenized Persian invasion which began in about 180 B.C. and was more or less absorbed by the Hindu culture; an Islamic invasion beginning in 711 A.D. which reached its peak with the attempt of Emperor Aurangzeb (1658-1707) to Islamicize the Moghul Empire; and the period of British imperialism which can be dated from December 31, 1600, when Queen Elizabeth granted a charter to the London East India Company, until 1947. Of these three, the longest and most lasting in effect was the Islamic invasion—primary basis for the British partition of India and Pakistan in 1947. The first two of these invasions came across land from the west; the third came from the sea. This helps to explain some of the quirks of religious demography on the subcontinent. Islam first consolidated in its invasion of the west, more than a quarter million square miles of arid territory not dissimilar in climate from its homeland. As the Moghuls extended their rule they relied more heavily on religious conversion to maintain support. Such converts were coopted into the new ruling class of India. The West Pakistanis claim that these later converts were usually drawn from the lower castes who saw in the Islamic social system an equality that could never be achieved under the tenets of Hinduism. This explains why the small, dark (racially "inferior") people of the northeast also were Muslim, while emphasizing the racial and cultural differences between the East and West Wings of the "Islamic State" of Pakistan.

The British arriving from the south were quick to see the Moghuls as their chief rivals for the control of the subcontinent. By

1857 they had established universities at Calcutta, Madras, and Bombay. They created a Hindu merchant class which, while never rivaling the Hindu principalities in wealth, achieved a dominant place in the political structure of the British Empire in India. The replacement of Muslims by Hindus in the British administrative system was not entirely punitive in nature, although the Sepoy Mutiny did trigger one such purge. Sir Sayyid Ahmad Khan (1817-98), one of the first leaders in the movement for "Islamic rights," maintained that the Muslims were slow in reconciling themselves to the fact that with the disappearance of the Moghul Empire their system of education, with Persian as the medium of instruction, could not help in obtaining administrative posts with the British government. (Sayeed, 1968: 21)

It is claimed by some that Sir Sayyid received his knighthood from Queen Victoria in 1879 for his successful efforts in keeping the Muslims from attending the Indian National Congress. While this is probably true, less personal reasons for opposing Muslim participation were also important. He argued that representative government, which implied majority rule, would be disastrous for the Muslim minority. In October 1906, 70 leading Muslims forming the "Simla deputation" under the leadership of the Aga Khan approached the Viceroy Lord Minto with a petition, granted immediately, which assured the Muslims a separate electorate and established the Muslim League. The stated aim of the Muslim League was "to promote among the Muslims of India a feeling of Loyalty to the British Government." (Ali, 1970: 26)

Islam never succeeded in consolidating its hold on the Indian subcontinent. This can be traced in part to a Hindu capacity for absorbing alien cultures while maintaining its own identity, but perhaps more directly to difficulties of communication and transportation. These had the effect of diminishing the government's effectiveness as the distance from the administrative capital increased. The British succeeded where the Moghul Empire failed largely because of the technology of the industrial revolution. The main contribution of the British to the subcontinent was to create an administrative infrastructure, a system of roads and railways, and a profound concommitant change in economic, social, and political patterns. There was also a 56 percent increase in population from 1880 to 1941 (Brown, 1958: 43). Still, the consolidation of the Indian empire was not achieved until 1877 when Queen Victoria was proclaimed Empress of India, and even then some remote areas remained out of effective administrative control for the remaining 70 years of British rule in India.

If the British succeeded in the administrative unification of the Indian continent, are they also to blame for its division? The predominant Indian view has been that the British had a conscious policy of divide and rule. Sangat Singh has presented a concise statement of this position:

> . . . the British visualized that India was bound to be free and, if united, would by its own right be a power to reckon with in Asia . . . to the detriment of Britain's global interests in the region. Hence, their sponsoring of the move for Pakistan as a sovereign independent state to watch their interests. (1970: 1-2)

Singh perceives this to be a pattern in British postimperial relations as well, arguing that the British set religion against religion and race against race in the Middle East, Cyprus, Malaysia (Singapore and Brunei), Ireland, and elsewhere (pp. 6-7). While the pattern of intranational strife in her former colonies is consistent enough to support the notion that Britain planted such fratricidal time bombs, it is difficult to believe that the British government could have acted with the degree of foresight required by this argument.

In a more limited and direct sense, however, the historical evidence supports the notion of a policy of divide and rule in the British Indian Empire. The British, recognizing the Moghul Empire as their chief rival for control of the subcontinent, first elevated the status of the Hindu population. When the demand for home rule became apparent, as early as the 1870s, they began to seek rapprochement with the Muslim landlords who represented a possible countervailing political force and who greatly feared Hindu dominance. Still these efforts seem to have been aimed not so much at emasculating an inevitably independent India as at preventing Indian independence and maintaining the Empire. To jump ahead a little in the chronology for further evidence, the only two alternatives offered to the Atlee government by Lord Wavell (Commander-in-Chief in India) at the time of Mountbatten's appointment as Viceroy, were a phased withdrawal first from the Congress-controlled areas and last from the areas which were eventually to become West Pakistan with power to be handed over on 31 March 1948, or the reestablishment of power and continued British rule for at least 15 years. (Sayeed, 1968: 165) The major concern at this time was that Britain might be held responsible for the "Balkanization" of India to the detriment of her continued economic interests in the region. In this, we can see that the alternative of withdrawal and its Balkanizing outcome was being used to argue against the ending of the imperial system. The ultimate selection of that alternative was not an expression of either an imperial or postimperial strategy.

THE FOUNDING OF PAKISTAN

The original idea for Pakistan was supposedly put forward in 1933 by Choudhary Rahmat Ali, a postgraduate student at Cambridge.

At the time it was characterized by Mohammad Ali Jinnah, later "father of Pakistan," as "a crazy scheme," and by the Aga Khan as "chimerical and impracticable" (Singh, 1970: 3). The work Pakistan meaning "land of the spiritually pure and clean" in Urdu was coined by Choudhary. It is composed of the letters of Islamic homelands: Punjab, Afghania (N.W. Frontier Province), Kashmir, Iran, Sind, Turkharistan, Afghanistan, and Baluchistan. Not all of these regions became part of Pakistan and, significantly, East Bengal, today's Bangladesh, was not included in Choudhary's original plan. Agitation for a separate state became more serious during the world wars.

In 1916 Jinnah had persuaded the Muslim League to cooperate with the Indian Congress in obtaining home rule, stipulating in the Lucknow Pact that the right of secession by Muslim provinces be guaranteed. The Lahore Resolution of 1940 which formalized the demand for Pakistan stated "that the areas in which the Muslims are numerically in the majority as in the northwestern and eastern zones of India should be grouped to constitute independent states in which constituent units shall be autonomous and sovereign." (cited in Jahan, 1972: 22). The resolution was amended in 1946 over the objections of Bengali Muslim leaders to call for a single state. The British Cabinet Mission Plans of 1941 and 1946 proposed an Indian Federation in which Muslims would hold a majority in two regional zones out of seven—the approximate ratio of Muslim to Hindu in the population. The Muslim League argued that this would seal their minority status. They would settle for nothing less than that the right of secession be guaranteed.

The partition of the Indian subcontinent was completed and Pakistan emerged as an independent nation on August 5, 1947. The British decision to allow the Maharajah of Kashmir, a Hindu in a province where the Muslim majority is four to one, to join India led to the October 19, 1947-to-July 29, 1949 Indo-Pakistani War and the complete breakdown of economic relations between the two new countries. Prior to partition, Pakistan and India had been economically interdependent for jute, cotton, wool, basic chemicals and coal, metals, electricity, and rubber. "Partition dismantled an elaborate economic infrastructure at a stroke." (Loshak, 1971: 9) Kashmir was an important economic prize to Pakistan as it would bring the necessary waterpower and irrigation that arid West Pakistan is without.

> Kashmir became at once the cornerstone and the keystone of its [Pakistan's] foreign policy where there was no foreign policy. And foreign policy, of course, determines defense policy. Kashmir is the chief reason why Pakistan has always maintained a large, strong army, and it is

> the size and influence of the army which has been the most
> important feature in Pakistan's political development.
> (p. 11)

By approximate measure, between 1946 and 1949 (the period leading up to the British retreat from India and including the first Indo-Pakistani War), over 2 million people died and 40 million relocated. The UN cease-fire in Kashmir granted most of the territory, including the water-rich Vale, to India, leaving Pakistan with only a small contiguous border strip. It also called for a popular vote to determine whether Kashmir would be part of India or Pakistan.

This set the tone of the relationship between India and Pakistan. The result of the war precluded economic cooperation and so determined the fate of the East Wing. In 1961 Peter Schmid wrote that "West Pakistan is an amputated limb, severed painfully, yet healing in the end. But East Pakistan is a piece of flesh cut from an organism carved out of the body of Bengal . . ." (p. 199) Out of the 1,414 industrial enterprises which Pakistan inherited at the time of partition only 314 were situated in East Bengal. (Ali, 1970: 37) Before partition three-fourths of the world's raw jute was grown in East Bengal, but all of the jute mills were located in a 60-mile strip along the Hooghly River north of Calcutta so that East Pakistan's main outlet for its major cash crop was blocked as a result of the 1947-49 war and its aftermath. In East Pakistan, Hindu landlords were, for the most part, replaced by West Pakistani Muslims and jute became a major source of Pakistani foreign exchange.

THE GROWTH OF EAST-WEST STRAINS IN PAKISTAN

In 1970 West Pakistan had a population of 61 million in an area of 310,000 square miles; it is made up of four provinces: Sind, Baluchistan, Afghania (N.W. Frontier Province), and Punjab, with Punjabis controlling most of the administration. East Pakistan, in 1970, had a population of 75 million in an area of 55,000 square miles. West Pakistan was more developed, with several major cities: Karachi (population 3 million), Lahore (2 million), Rawalpindi, the provisional capital, and Islamabad, the official capital, where most major construction was completed in 1971. East Bengal has only one major city, Dacca, with a population of 2 million. Yet, of the amount allocated for development between 1948 and 1951 only 22.1 percent went to East Pakistan which had the majority of the population and more backward conditions, and had contributed more to the Pakistani treasury than the sum of the entire development budget in both wings for the same years. By 1955 the percentage of development funds allocated to East Pakistan dropped to 12.6 percent of the total. Per capita income in West Pakistan rose from Rs. 330 in 1950 to Rs. 373 in 1960 while in East Pakistan during the same period per capita income declined from Rs. 305 to Rs. 288. By 1968, 66 percent of all industrial profits, 97 percent of the insurance funds and 80 percent of the banks were controlled by about 20 families in West Pakistan (Jahan, 1972: 60).

The first signs of dissatisfaction in East Bengal appeared only a few months after partition in February 1948 and were provoked by the decision to impose Urdu, as the official national language, upon Pakistan. Language was the central concern of the demonstrations at Dacca University on February 21, 1952, which spread into a province-wide strike after a number of students were killed by the military. The recognition of Bengali as a national language was one of the points in the 21-point program which brought a sweeping electoral victory to the United Front in 1954. The language controversy is an outstanding example of the blanket application of a policy which might be useful for the four provinces of the West Wing, but which was detrimental to the East. In the West over 60 percent of the population spoke Punjabi but sizable minorities spoke Sindhi, Pushtu and Urdu so that the imposition of a single national language made some sense, but in East Bengal more than 98 percent of the population spoke Bengali. Since the majority of the Pakistani population was Bengali it could be argued that if a single national language were required it should be Bengali.

Bengalis perceived the language and economic policies as a reflection of Punjabi determination to maintain East Bengal as a colony of the West Wing. Even more importantly, the flood-washed Bengalis did not share the West Pakistani interest in Kashmir, which, moreover, prevented the normalization of relations with India essential to Bengali development. One hundred sixty-two members of the East Pakistani Assembly denounced the U.S.-Pakistan Bilateral Aid Pact—the Pact was signed after the central government dissolved the Legislative Assembly of East Pakistan and proclaimed governor's rule on May 30, 1954. The SEATO and CENTO Pacts of 1954 and 1955 were concluded without any input from the East Wing, which remained under the direct rule of Governor General Iskandar Mirza.

It is claimed by Bengalis that the "One Unit Bill" passed in 1954 was aimed at neutralizing the power of the majority population in East Bengal. It is true that the Bengali Assembly, being dissolved, did not vote on the bill which specified that the East and West Wings would have equal representation in the National Assembly. But the Sind Assembly, in West Pakistan, was surrounded by armed police to insure that it voted for One Unit. At this time, the major opposition movement in the West aimed at the creation of six semiautonomous provinces. General Ayub Khan, who became defense minister in 1954, claimed that the prime minister, Mohammed Ali Borga, gave him at the same time documents authorizing the army to take over the country and Ayub to produce a new constitution. (Kahn, 1967: 52) He chose to wait until October, 1958 and, at first, the army was greeted as a savior from the corruption and incompetence of the provincial political elites.

One of the major problems of West Pakistan was the lack of any viable political infrastructure. It is a feudal system overlaid with a military bureaucracy. In East Pakistan the situation is quite different. The Bengalis (of both East and West Bengal) have a tradition of being highly political and of leftist leanings. Politics is organized at the village level, and students and unions have provided a significant input. The 1954 victory of the United Front provides an example of the successful political organization in East Pakistan. The central government was faced with a twofold problem of building a viable political elite in West Pakistan, while holding the East in check. This was done by police repression, chiefly arrest and exile, as well as by coercion and dissolution of provincial assemblies. It was also found useful to exclude students from politics. An order issued by the Education Ministry prior to the elections of 1965 illustrates this last tactic:

> . . . in regard to educational institutions receiving financial assistance from the government, a condition of grant should be that the institutions concerned will frame rules and regulations on their own initiative to ensure that the employees whether serving on whole-time or part-time basis [this includes all students receiving grants and loans] will not offer themselves as candidates in any election . . . (Ali, 1970: 125)

Government employees are also excluded, and, since there was almost no entrepreneurial class, the effect was to bar most of the literate population from political participation.

THE CRISIS

The 1965 Indo-Pakistani War had several consequences. Internally, it elevated the pro-Peking faction of the National Awami Party led by Maulana Bhashani. The National Awami Party in 1966 and afterward helped the regime to curb demands for Bengali autonomy.

BANGLADESH: THE PRICE OF NATIONAL UNITY

It led Bhutto to launch the People's Party, and it demonstrated to East Pakistan its isolation from and value to the West Wing.

> When during a foreign affairs debate in the National Assembly in March 1966, members from East Pakistan specifically asked why 75 million people of East Pakistan were exposed to Indian threat for the sake of 5 million Kashmiris, Foreign Minister Bhutto replied that India could not raise her little finger at East Pakistan because of the threat from China. East Pakistanis naturally felt that if their safety really depended upon the good graces of the Chinese, and fortuitous circumstances of the Sino-Indian conflict, why should they continue to accept the domination of the Western Wing? (Nat'l Assembly of Pakistan, Debates, March 15, 1966: 488-89, cited in Singh, 1970: 5)

Externally and internally the war left Pakistan in a state of chaos. Martial law was maintained from the time of the war until February 17, 1969, when disorders and, finally, a general strike convinced Ayub he should not stand for reelection. At the time of Ayub's decision to resign, both the current leaders of Pakistan and Bangladesh were in jail charged with a part in the same conspiracy. In a meeting on March 13, 1969, President Ayub agreed with them to restore parliamentary government and to hold direct elections based on universal adult suffrage. On March 23, 1969, General Yahya Khan took over the government, and again proclaimed martial law, promising to hold elections within 18 months. Political campaigning went on for more than a year with the elections postponed twice: on August 16, due to widespread flooding in East Pakistan and on November 12 when a cyclone killed an estimated 500,000 people in East Pakistan—a grim reminder of the neglect of development projects in the East Wing.

Sheikh Mujibur Rahman campaigned on a "Six Point Program" first published in 1966 under the title "Our Right to Live" it contained the following provisions:

1. The establishment of a federal form of government, with a parliament to be the supreme point of power, directly elected by universal adult suffrage.
2. The federal government would control only defense and foreign policy, leaving all other subjects to the federating states of East and West Pakistan.
3. The two wings would have separate (but freely convertible currencies) or if one currency, separate fiscal policies to prevent the flight of capital from East to West Pakistan.

4. The federal government would have no power of taxation. It would share state taxes for the needs of foreign and defense affairs.
5. Each of the federating states would have the power to enter into trade agreements with foreign countries. They would also have full control over their earned foreign exchange.
6. The states would have their own militias or paramilitary forces.

Most of the factions of East Bengal coalesced around these demands and Mujib's Awami League. A certain drag was put upon the movement by the pro-Peking faction of the National Awami Party led by the Maulana Bhashani. This large and important faction (Bhashani is an old peasant leader, originally cofounder of the Awami League and remains Mujib's major opponent today) could not endorse anything as drastic as the Six Points because China supported a strong united Pakistan as a buffer against India. Bhashani's party boycotted the election.

Even though Mujib publicly disavowed this intention, claiming all that was desired was a measure of autonomy, the acceptance of the Six Points would have undermined the existing nation-state. The second, fourth, fifth and sixth points would have radically changed the relations of the provinces and certainly turned Pakistan onto a more neutralist course, as well as undermining the control of the army by removing its direct access to funds. It would no longer be expected under the Six Points that the army could have held to the myth of the eventual military "liberation" of Kashmir, and the provincial militias could be expected to take over much of the army's role in the maintenance of order in the provinces.

The first point was accepted before the general election of 1970. With regard to the sixth point, the North West Frontier Province and Baluchistan currently have their own paramilitary organizations under the Awami Party. In this sense, the Six Points were a recognition of the facts of life. On the other hand, their blanket application would have created a radically different kind of nation-state; one that might not be counted upon in any kind of power balance involving the USSR and India on one side and the United States and China on the other. China needed the U.S. presence in Pakistan as a buffer for its two enemies, the USSR and India. Had Mujib's plan been accepted, Pakistan would no longer be in a position to play its pivotal role in the U.S.-Chinese connection—a role which Fulbright has noted allowed it to accept aid from both the United States and China for one purpose while redirecting that aid into its conflict with India (cited in Bhutto, 1969: 57) and ultimately into the attempt at genocide in East Bengal.

Pakistan's first "one man, one vote" election was held on December 7, 1970. It resulted in a clear majority for Mujib's Awami League in East Pakistan which won 151 out of 153 seats contested.

At the same time, Bhutto's People's Party won 81 out of 138 seats in West Pakistan. The overall result of the election was not just to demonstrate the Awami League's hold on the East, but to give it an absolute majority in the new Pakistani Assembly. The purpose of the Assembly, according to President Yahya Kahn's charge to it, was to draw up a constitution for Pakistan within 120 days of its first meeting. If it failed to do so, it was to be dissolved and new elections held, and the process presumably was to be repeated until a constitution emerged.

The crisis presented by the victory of the Awami League generated a flurry of activity aimed at trying to reach an agreement and avoid direct confrontation. Mujib had campaigned on the Six Points as a precondition to the formulation of a new constitution. Now, ironically, having obtained an absolute majority in the new assembly, despite the fact that it was a transitional body, Mujib had the clear prospect of becoming the next prime minister of Pakistan. In fact, on December 17, 1970, he was described by President Yahya Kahn as "Pakistan's next Prime Minister," and this would presumably have meant a Pakistan controlled by the East rather than the West Wing. The Six Points, on the other hand, would have resulted in the fragmentation of the existing united Pakistan into five, or more, parts, effectively throwing away the fruits of his electoral dominance over all Pakistan. Nonetheless, Mujib refused to take part in the Assembly unless the Six Points were accepted by the West Pakistanis.

Negotiations over the agenda of the new National Assembly continued from January through March while Yahya prepared what can, without melodrama, be called his "final solution" to the Bengali problem. Prior to January 1971 there was a force of approximately 40,000 West Pakistani soldiers in East Bengal. The logistical demands faced by West Pakistan in attempting a campaign of military repression and occupation in East Bengal were immense, and, as later events were to show, practically impossible in the face of opposition. Between January and March of 1971, a further force of 20,000 troops in civilian dress were ferried by air from Karachi to Dacca. This in itself was no small undertaking since the direct airlanes to East Bengal over India had been closed to Pakistan since 1970 as a result of the highjacking of an Indian Airlines plane to Lahore. The plane had been blown up and no compensation was paid to the Indian government. The closure of the direct airlanes meant that Pakistani planes were forced to fly around the southern tip of India, keeping over international waters. This trebled the distance involved between West Pakistan and East Bengal. Seaborne supplies had to travel the same 3000 miles to reach the East Bengal port of Chittagong.

It is not clear whether the negotiations were all sham. Late in February 1971 Bhutto, whose electoral victory had given him leadership in the West, announced he would boycott the National Assembly.

This prompted Yahya to postpone the first session which had been scheduled for March 7th. This, in turn, sparked spontaneous demonstrations in East Bengal. At one point in late March Yahya is supposed to have worked out a compromise which granted autonomy based on the Six Points to East Pakistan while withholding application of the Six Points to the other four provinces of the West, pending a constitution which would be drafted by separate committees from the East and West (Jahan, 1972: 195). The effect of such a settlement would have been to acknowledge the eventual independence of the East while preserving the West wing. Bhutto denounced this as a sellout. While the Awami League waited for official announcement of the settlement, the Pakistani army attacked the campus of the University of Dacca, the headquarters of the East Pakistani Rifles and police, offices of the Awami League, and newspapers without warning on the night of March 25th.

THE CIVIL/INTERNATIONAL CONFLICT
AND THE BIRTH OF BANGLADESH

The military government had woefully miscalculated the cost and effectiveness of the "pacification" of East Bengal. On June 28 in a radio address Yahya declared "Our exports have sharply declined . . . collection of taxes has suffered . . . we have to use our resources with much greater restraint . . . a thorough revision of the import policy. . . inessential items banned. . . maximum austerity." His own words were a direct contradiction of his initial statement that Pakistan had returned to normal as of March 27th. Conscription, introduced in July, brought West Pakistani forces in East Bengal to 80,000. Still the Mukti Bahini grew stronger, blowing up roads and bridges, three power stations in Dacca, and even damaging the Intercontinental Hotel. In August the direct cost of military intervention was placed at $2,184,000 a day, and it was estimated that a force of 250,000 trained men would be needed to put an end to guerrilla activities (cited in Loshak, 1971: 119).

In July 1971 President Yahya threatened to declare a general war on India for her part in harboring Mukti forces and for supplying them with small arms and explosives. It is difficult to estimate how much direct aid the Indians supplied; as the flood of refugees reached 10 million, Indian denunciations of Pakistan and calls for action in the global community became more frequent. Indian ratification of the Soviet treaty in August made Pakistani fears more acute. Emphasizing the Indian threat was useful to Yahya in promoting cohesion in West Pakistan where, according to Yahya's own admission, the government's position, both political and economic, was worsening day by day. Loshak speculates in his book, which was in press prior to the outbreak of the war, that Pakistan might precipitate a war with India even knowing that it could not win. His reasoning was that the Pakistani government might feel that such a war would bring swift major-power intervention to stop the fighting, and would impose another Tashkent-type settlement which would leave East Bengal's status unchanged (1971: 128).

It is quite possible that the Mukti Bahini could have held out and eventually won a protracted war of national liberation in the absence of military intervention by the Indians. However, with a protracted struggle, the Indian government had to fear the spillover of guerrilla activities into the already highly politicized environment of West Bengal. In the absence of any outside interest in preventing the continuation of atrocities that had been fully reported in the world press for eight months preceding the war, India could be expected to rescue Bangladesh as soon as the Himalayan passes were closed to China. China had made an emergency advance of $211 million on an interest-free loan to Pakistan in May of 1971. By waiting until December, India offered China a reasonable excuse for nonintervention even if the Chinese commitment to Pakistan had been perceived to require such action. In quieting a destabilizing situation in East Bengal, India could expect the tacit approval of the major powers the U.S. "tilt" to Pakistan, to the contrary, notwithstanding. India took 73,000 Pakistani soldiers in East Bengal prisoner and captured 2,500 square miles of Punjab and Sind provinces in the west for good measure.

BANGLADESH: THE CONSERVATIVE SOLUTION?

In a <u>Foreign Affairs</u> article published soon after the Bangladesh crisis had been settled by the Indo-Pakistani war of December 3-17, 1971, Phillips Talbott argued

> Actually two separate sets of principles are involved in the policies of India and the US in this instance. India assessed the Bangladesh issue in terms of Wilsonian self-determination. The US government chose to stand on the concepts built into the U.N. Charter that protected the sovereignty and integrity of member nations against interference by external powers. (1972: 708-9)

However, even he was forced to admit that the flood of refugees to India had effectively internationalized the problem and undermined the U.S. position. Even granting the U.S. position, the principle laid down in the UN charter does not seem to require the supplying of a "magic pipeline" from which arms and equipment continued to flow to the Pakistani military long after a cutoff had been imposed despite the objections of the people and Congress of the United States. The U.S. concerns were more pragmatic and global. A memo of December 4 from the Washington Special Action Group (an elite subunit of the NSC) leaked to Jack Anderson and published in the New York Times on January 6, 1972, offers some insight:

> According to Dr. Kissinger the only move left to us at the present time is to make clear our position relative to our greater strategy. Everyone knows how all this will come out and everyone knows that India will ultimately occupy East Pakistan.

Kissinger's visits to Pakistan, where he was supposedly searching for a political settlement, turned out to have been a cover for negotiations with Peking preparatory to the U.S.-China rapprochement Bhutto had predicted in his 1969 book (pp. 133-34).

The Bangladesh crisis also marked China's loss of innocence as an international actor for pragmatic and strategic considerations won out over ideology. It had long been maintained by Bengali radicals that China's friendship for the military dictatorships of Ayub and Yahya was undermining the revolution. In the introduction of his book Tariq Ali had declared

> Even if the Chinese government tells us that there is not a revolutionary situation we will disagree with them. We know there is a revolutionary situation and we will exploit it. We will not let our generation rot. (1970: 22).

Of course, it would not do to have a hostile Pakistan on China's borders, nor would it do to have Pakistan swallowed up by India. But to deny the inevitability of Bengali national liberation was a significant misreading of the Maoist view of history. A pro-Peking Bangladesh would have also put some logistical pressure on the Indian province of Assam and provided the opportunity to promote a revolutionary secessionist movement both there and in West Bengal. It can be seen, in retrospect, that this outcome could have eventuated if Pakistan had been forced by the astronomical costs of her adventure in East Bengal to grant the radical autonomy agreed upon in the negotiations of March 20. Pakistan could not have borne this cost for over nine months without aid from the United States and China.

> The US, in principle, supported unity and was opposed to secession. There are a lot of areas in the world where secession, if spotted and if it were to become a way of life could be very, very dangerous to the rest of the world.

This statement, by then Secretary of State William P. Rogers in his year-end news conference (reported in the New York Times of January 7, 1972), is, in a more simplistic and normative vein, reminiscent of Hoffman's previously mentioned concern over the fragmentation of the world. On surveying the recent threats to world peace one can ask, with some justification, whether it is not the maintenance of unviable nation-state units that poses the real threat. Jahan's analysis of the failure of national integration in Pakistan indicates that Ayub's emphasis on "state-building"—creating strong central institutions at the expense of national political development—was dictated by the international environment. Pakistan's defense policy precluded economic cooperation with India and thereby left East Bengal a colony of the West Wing. The East Bengali elite responded with a demand for autonomy which was eventually met by a military policy calculated to destroy the Bengali will effectively for generations. It was the imposition of the military policy, as Jahan notes, which finally changed Bengali nationalism from an elite to a mass phenomenon. By that time there was no alternative to nationalism.

SOURCES

Ali, Tariq. Pakistan: Military Rule or People's Power. New York: Wm. Morrow, 1970.

Beg, Aziz. Pakistan Faces India. Lahore: Babur & Amer Publications, 1967.

Bhargava, Ganti Suryanarayana. Pakistan in Crisis. 2nd ed. Delhi: Vikas Publications, 1971.

Bhutto, Zulfikar Ali. The Myth of Independence. London: Oxford University Press, 1969.

Bowles, Chester. Promises to Keep: My Years in Public Life: 1941-1969. New York: Harper & Row, 1969.

Brown, W. Norman. *The United States, India, and Pakistan.* Cambridge: Harvard University Press, 1958.

Chanana, Charanjit. *Economics of Bangladesh.* New Delhi: Marketing and Economic Research Bureau, 1971.

Chaudhri, Mohammed Ahsen. *Pakistan and the Great Powers.* Karachi: Council for Pakistan Studies, 1970.

———. *Pakistan and the Regional Pacts.* (texts) Karachi: East Pub, 1960.

Chaudhri, Muhammad Ali. *The Emergence of Pakistan.* New York: Columbia University Press, 1967.

Choudhury, G. W. *The Last Days of United Pakistan.* Bloomington, Ind.: Indiana University Press, 1975.

Deutsch, Karl W. *Nationalism and Its Alternatives.* New York: Knopf, 1969.

Hodson, H. V. *The Great Divide: Britain—India—Pakistan.* New York: Atheneum, 1971.

Hoffman, Stanley. "Obstinate or Obsolete? The Fate of the Nation-State and the Case of Western Europe." In *International Regionalism: Readings*, ed. J. S. Nye, pp. 177-230. Boston: Little, Brown, 1968.

Hussain, Arif. *Pakistan: Its Ideology and Foreign Policy.* London: Frank Cass & Co., 1966.

Jahan, Rounaq. *Pakistan: Failure in National Integration.* New York: Columbia University Press, 1972.

Kahn, Mohammed Ayub. *Friends Not Masters—A Political Autobiography.* Cambridge: Oxford University Press, 1967.

Lewis, Stephen R. *Pakistan: Industrialization and Trade Policies.* Paris: OECD, Cambridge: Oxford University Press, 1970.

Loshak, David. *Pakistan Crisis.* London: Heinemann, 1971.

Mankekar, D. R. *Twenty-Two Fateful Days: Pakistan Cut to Size.* Bombay, New York: Paragon, 1967.

Mankekar, D.R. *Pakistan Colonialism in East Pakistan*. Bombay: Somaiya Publishers, 1971.

Mascarenhas, Anthony. *The Rape of Bangla Desh*. Delhi: Vikas Publishers, 1971.

Maxwell, Neville. *India's China War*. New York: Pantheon Books, 1970.

Pakistan Central Statistics Office. *20 Years of Pakistan in Statistics*. Karachi: Manager of Publications, 1968.

Permanent Mission of India to the UN. "The Issue: Rule by Ballot. The Answer: Reign of Terror; A Grim Chronicle of the 72 Million People of East Pakistan." New York, 1971.

Salzberg, John. "UN Prevention of Human Rights Violations: The Bangladesh Case," *International Organization* 27, no. 1 (Winter 1973): 115-27.

Sayeed, Khalid B. *Pakistan: The Formative Phase*. 2nd ed. London: Oxford University Press, 1968.

Schanberg, Sydney H. "Pakistan Divided," *Foreign Affairs* (October 1971): 125-35.

Schmid, Peter. *India, Mirage and Reality*. London, 1961.

Singh, Sangat. *Pakistan's Foreign Policy: An Appraisal*. Delhi: National Printing Works, 1970.

Talbot, Phillips. "Subcontinent Menage a Trois," *Foreign Affairs* (July 1972): 698-710.

U.S. Congress. Senate. Committee on the Judiciary. Subcommittee Investigating Problems Connected with Refugees and Escapees. *Crisis in South Asia: A Report by Sen. Edward Kennedy*. Washington, D.C.: U.S. Government Printing Office, November 1, 1971.

——. House. Committee on Foreign Affairs. Subcommittee on Asian and Pacific Affairs. *Crisis in East Pakistan: Hearings, Ninety-Second Congress, First Session*. Washington, D.C.: U.S. Government Printing Office, 1971.

Vakil, C. N. *Economic Consequences of Divided India*. Bombay, 1950.

Zaman, M. R. *Why the Bengalees Are Fighting for an Independent Bangla Desh*. Ithaca, New York, 1971.

ABOUT THE EDITOR AND CONTRIBUTORS

RAY EDWARD JOHNSTON chairs the International Studies Association's INTERNET on Divided Nations, and is an associate professor of political science at Wayne State University. He is a coauthor of A Primer of Political Analysis (1968), and is a contributor to numerous journals including the Journal of International Affairs and the Urban and Social Change Review. He has served as a consultant to the U.S. Department of Health, Education, and Welfare, and was director of Project Upward-Bound at Purdue University from 1965 to 1967. He has been a visiting professor in the Republic of Korea and in the Republic of China, and he is currently engaged in research on the comparative foreign policies of divided nations.

THOMAS E. HACHEY is an associate professor of history at Marquette University. Among his publications are The Problem of Partition: Peril to World Peace (1972), and Voices of Revolution: Rebels and Rhetoric (1973). He is presently completing research on the Irish issue in British politics from 1914 to 1922.

ARTHUR M. HANHARDT, JR. is a professor of political science at the University of Oregon. He is a specialist on Germany and has written on the socialization of German youth, the integration of East and West Germany, and German democracy. He has contributed to a number of journals, including the American Behavioral Scientist, the Journal of International Affairs, and Koelner Zeitschrift fur Sozeialologie-Psychologie. During the past few years he has been presenting his research at a number of professional conferences. His book entitled The German Democratic Republic was published in 1968.

YOUNG WHAN KIHL is a professor of political science at Iowa State University, and a specialist in international relations and Asian politics. Among the journals to which he often contributes are Asian Survey, the Journal of Korean Affairs, and the Korean Journal of International Studies. He has held grants from the Social Science Research Council in 1966 and 1973, and a Fulbright-Hayes Senior Research Fellowship in Korea, also in 1973.

KATHLEEN KNIGHT is a candidate for a doctoral degree in political science at the University of California, Los Angeles. She is a member of the Divided Nations INTERNET of the International Studies Association, and holds a Regents Fellowship at the University of California.

RICHARD L. MERRITT is a professor of political science at the University of Illinois at Urbana-Champaign. He has served on the editorial boards of the American Political Science Review and the Midwest Journal of Politics, and his work often appears in numerous other professional journals. His books include Symbols of the American Community, 1735-1775 (1966), and Systematic Approaches to Comparative Politics (1970). He has edited Comparing Nations (1966), and Communication in International Politics (1972).

YUNG WEI is a professor of political science at Memphis State University and a member of the INTERNET on Divided Nations and Political Partition. He is currently Deputy Director of the Institute of International Relations, Taipei. He has specialized in empirical theory and methodology in the fields of political behavior, Chinese political systems, political development, comparative elites, and international political behavior. He is a contributor to Polity, Annals of the Chinese Political Association, Encyclopedia of Social Sciences (Taipei), and The Oriental. Among his books are Communist China: A System-Functional Reader (1972), The Nature and Methods of Social Sciences (Taipei, 1971), and The Modernization of a Chinese Society: Taiwan's Path to Development (Praeger, 1977).

RELATED TITLES
Published by
Praeger Special Studies

SMALL STATES AND SEGMENTED SOCIETIES:
National Political Integration in a Global Environment
 edited by Stephanie G. Neuman

*SOUTH ASIAN CRISIS: INDIA, PAKISTAN, AND
BANGLADESH: A Political and Historical Analysis
of the 1971 War
 Robert Jackson

COLONIAL EMANCIPATION IN THE PACIFIC AND
THE CARIBBEAN: A Legal and Political Analysis
 Arnold H. Leibowitz

CIVIL WARS AND THE POLITICS OF INTERNATIONAL
RELIEF: Africa, South Asia, and the Caribbean
 edited by Morris Davis

*For sale in the United States and Philippines only